Training Your Rottweiler

Second Edition

Barbara L. McNinch

BARRON'S

About the Author

Since the first edition of this book in 1999, Barb co-founded Ringtime Training Center in Burgaw, NC where she taught private behavior modification sessions, puppy class, and competition obedience classes. Barb also worked in tandem with Wrightsville Beach Pet Hospital as a behavioral specialist, increasing her knowledge of behaviors such as separation anxiety, aggression, and other canine issues.

She is currently a volunteer with a new program in Pender County called Positive Pets Prison Program. The program evaluates dogs from the local shelters. The dogs are then placed into the prison and trained by the inmates. The dogs are trained to the level of CGC and then placed with new owners.

In 2004, Barb won the Dog Writer's Association and Off-Lead Magazine's special award for Best Training Article on the Web. The article can be found at the following web site: *http://www.myrottweilerpups.com/page11.html*.

Barb currently owns two dogs, Rottweiler, Esmonds Go for Broke (Broker), and a Cardigan Welsh Corgi, Tell Tails Dare to Bare. Eight and a half year old Broker has his CD, Herding Instinct Certificate, and CGC. Tell Tails Dare to Bare is two years old and has her Herding Instinct and is currently working in agility and obedience.

All inquiries should be addressed to:
Barron's Educational Series, Inc.
250 Wireless Boulevard
Hauppauge, NY 11788
www.barronseduc.com

ISBN: 978-0-7641-4098-3

Library of Congress Control No. 2008939527

Printed in China
9 8 7 6 5 4

Acknowledgments

The author wishes to thank the following contributors to this book.

Sharyl Mayhew, of Precious Dog Training and Rescue for allowing the use of her beginning cart training article from her extensive web site; Colette and Warrick Wilson for the use of their article "Carting With Your Dog, Frequently Asked Questions," from their web site; Jan cooper, who granted permission and access to use all of the information on Rottweiler legislation and laws found in Chapter 14; the American Rottweiler Club for allowing use of the educational materials from their web site; the American Kennel Club for use of the Canine Good Citizen testing information from their web site; Lisa McLain for photographing the training slides.

Finally, thanks to Wendy and Jack Volhard for the use of their Puppy Aptitude Test.

In addition, I would like to acknowledge and thank my colleague at Ringtime Training Center for the wonderful opportunity to work and learn over the years. This work has afforded me the blackboard on which to draw and the experience for much of this book. Our relationship and friendship means more to me than I can express.

Thank you to everyone, everywhere, who told me that I must do this, I could do this, and that I should do this . . . I did.

Cover Credits

Shutterstock: front cover; Cheryl Ertelt: back cover, inside front cover, and inside back cover.

Photo Credits

Tara Darling: page 44; Cheryl Ertelt: pages 2, 10, 13, 19, 34, 51 (top), 53 (right), 55 (bottom), 56, 57, 63, 65, 66, 73, 89, 100, 103, 104, and 108; Kent Akselsen: pages viii, 45, 67, and 98; Jean M. Fogle: pages 75, 77, 79, 80, 82, and 86; Karen Hudson: pages 32 (left), 59 (bottom), and 85; Isabelle Francais: pages 4, 7, 39, 87, and 91; Frantino@PetProfiles: pages 20 and 40; Paulette Johnson: pages 12, 30 (bottom), 31, 32 (right), 37, 59 (top), 71, 95, and 97; Lisa McLain: pages 24, 25, 26, 27, 30 (top), 33, 43, 46, 51 (bottom), 53 (left), 54, 55 (top), 58, 64, and 72; Pets by Paulette: pages 8, 11, 35, and 38; Darci Proctor: page 5; Connie Summers/Paulette Johnson: page 69.

Contents

1 Introduction 1

2 Getting to Know the Rottweiler 3

Character and Personality Traits 3
Finding a Rottweiler 5
Choosing the Right Puppy 7
Puppies' Developmental Stages 8
Puppy Aptitude Test (PAT) 9

3 Starting the Training Program 17

The Importance of a Social Life 17
Children and Rottweilers 18
Safety Measures to Take to Prevent Bites 20

Learning to Teach and Making It Fun   *21*

Operant Conditioning and How It
  Aids Training   21
Daily Training Moments   24
Handling and Submission Exercises   25
Leadership: The Key to Success   27

Training Tools   *29*

Leash and Collar   29
Toys   31
Treats   33
Timing   34
Talking   34
Tug-O-War   35

First Lessons and Handling Problems   *36*

Teaching the Name   36
Collar and Leash Training   37
Crate-Training   38
House-Training   41
Biting   42
Chewing   44
Grooming and Handling   45
Jumping Up   46

7 *Obedience Exercises* 48

Attention, Please	48
Walking on a Loose Lead	51
The *Stay* Exercises	52
Come-When-Called: The Recall Game	60

8 *AKC Obedience* 62

Overview	62
Exercises	62
Home Schooling	68

9 *Canine Good Citizen Test* 70

Overview and Purpose	70
The Ten Tests	71
Home Schooling	74

10 *Agility Training* 75

Overview and Purpose	75
Home Schooling	76

11 Carting 78

Fundamentals	78
Terms	78
Equipment	78
Vehicle Types	79
Harness Types	80
Home Schooling	81

12 Additional Activities for You and Your Rottweiler 84

Conformation	84
Tracking	86
Herding	87
Therapy Work	88
Schutzhund Training	88
Rally Obedience	89

13 Aggression 90

The Reasons Behind the Aggression	90
Handling the Aggressive Outburst	92
Teaching a *Quiet* Command	94

14

Rescued Rottweilers 96

Unscrupulous Breeders 96
A Helping Hand 96
Training Advice to Use for Rescued
  Rottweilers 98
Legislative Issues Concerning Rottweilers 99
What You Can Do 100

Useful Addresses and Literature 102

Glossary 106

Index 110

1 *Introduction*

I had two goals when I wrote this book: The first was to supply the many Rottweiler fanciers out there with a solid foundation for handling and training their personal pet dog. Based on what I knew of the breed, as well as what I know about dogs, I felt that some methods do not work well for any dog, let alone the Rottweiler.

After 25 years of instructing pet dog owners and handling and training my own dogs, I wanted to share a kinder, gentler type of training. This training is based on teaching the dog leadership first and obedience second. I wanted a book that average owners can use to educate themselves regarding the behavior of Rottweilers—not a book on pedigrees, or breeders.

With this in mind, I must explain that the order in which you will be introduced to methods may seem strange to you. Keep in mind that the philosophy behind the training method is this: Establish leadership and learn the ideas behind the method first, then teach the dog basic obedience.

In Chapter 2 you will first learn some behavioral and personality characteristics of the Rottweiler, followed by some information on finding a Rottweiler and information on the developmental stages

of all pups. This information is key to understanding behavior; understanding behavior helps you become a better trainer and owner.

In Chapter 3 you'll learn some basic safety measures.

As you read on, in Chapter 4 you'll learn more about the method known as *operant conditioning*, and how to incorporate handling and training into daily life with the puppy, then you'll read about the leadership philosophy. This is all necessary for your attitude toward training itself as well as your attitude toward your Rottweiler.

Chapter 5 supplies a list of the important tools you will need in training. When you understand the range of tools you have at your disposal, you'll be better able to use the training method explained here.

Before you start obedience basics, get through puppyhood; use your new attitude and philosophy to teach the puppy lessons of behavior. The rules of the household come before anything else. This is all found in Chapter 6.

Once your Rottweiler is working with you for all the right reasons, then the obedience training will begin. You'll find you have a much more willing partner as

Rottweilers are large and powerful as well as highly intelligent animals.

ence you learn in this book, followed and practiced on a regular basis, is a perfect start to educating your Rottie in one or more of the activities listed.

If you do run into trouble with your Rottweiler, Chapter 13 will help. All the information in this chapter is based on the assumption that you are using the behavior and training methods already described in the previous chapters of this book. You cannot expect to solve problems without the tools, attitude, and understanding found in those chapters.

Finally, my second goal in writing this book was to provide rescue information as well as breed-specific legislative news. In Chapter 14 you'll find out about these issues as they pertain to the Rottweiler. This information is important to current as well as future owners of the breed.

Well-trained Rottweilers will help to represent the breed as worthy of ownership. Knowledge of rescue and legislation will allow all of us to help the breed. The more people who involve themselves in these two areas of ownership, the more education will become available to everyone. Learning about current laws and understanding the plight of Rottweilers that have been abandoned and abused will help you to educate others—in your neighborhood, your town, and even your state. Who knows—your well-trained Rottweiler might be the next ambassador for the breed in your city.

you work through the exercises discussed in Chapter 7.

Chapters 8 through 12 give you a clear picture of the many events and activities available for you to participate in with your Rottweiler. Each one is different and experts in each field are usually necessary to help guide you into the activity you choose; however, some Home Schooling is provided where applicable to help you get started on your own. The basic obedi-

2 Getting to Know the Rottweiler

Character and Personality Traits

The Rottweiler is a working breed, originally bred to herd cattle and to guard its owner at the marketplace. This is a large, powerful dog with the ability to take care of itself and its family. The well-bred Rottweiler can and will do its job with a calm confidence and, for the most part, with a willing attitude.

There are many Rottweilers in this country, some of them from suspect backgrounds. Rottweilers are often bought for the wrong reasons by the wrong people. They are not given enough *socialization*, and are then expected to understand that their job is to protect a home or person.

The Rottweiler is one of the most misunderstood breeds in America today; it is all too true that the breed can become dangerous and unpredictable in the wrong situation, but before the entire breed is condemned, an examination of why aggressive behaviors occur may help to clear the Rottweiler name.

If you're thinking of owning a Rottweiler, think about why you want the dog. If you think that good manners, liking children, or guarding the house will come naturally to

the Rottweiler, think again. The Rottweiler will not arrive in your house knowing how to behave; however, if you have the time to teach the dog good manners, socialize him to children, and *bond* with him, you are on the right track in owning this breed.

Before bringing home your new Rottweiler, learn about the tools of training and the philosophy behind some of the methods discussed in this book. Arming yourself with these tools before you bring the puppy home will prevent frustration for the whole family.

What's in There?

Behind the Rottweiler's big brown eyes is an extremely intelligent animal with personality and character traits that can amuse and frustrate you. While individual dogs are different, Rottweilers do seem

> **NOTE**
>
> *In this book, we have chosen to name our male dog Fritz and our female Mollie, in order to avoid the awkward use of the pronoun "it." We will alternate between the male and female dog to show that no sexism is intended.*

3

Although each dog is different, Rottweilers do share certain behavior traits.

to share certain characteristics and owners from all over the world relate the same stories regarding the behaviors of their pets.

The one common trait of Rottweilers is the grumble. This is a low growling coming from deep in the throat of the dog, which often occurs when he is being petted and hugged and is somewhat surprising when you first hear it. This grumbling sound is usually harmless and simply means that Fritz is enjoying himself. Naturally, any snapping and biting accompanied by growling or snarling are not acceptable behaviors. Another common behavior of Rottweilers everywhere is flip-

ping over on the back with all four feet in the air. They assume this position for a variety of reasons: One relates to being rubbed on the belly, and this is the most common time to hear them grumbling; also, Rottweilers often sleep with all four feet in the air and propped against a wall or piece of furniture. When playing with a toy they particularly love, they will flip into the position and literally hold the item between their paws; thus, they will admire it from a distance, bring it to their mouth to chew a bit, and then once again thrust it out to admire it. Anyone who owns a Rottweiler will tell you that this is a common scene around the house.

Finding a Rottweiler

The task of finding a mentally and physically sound Rottweiler doesn't have to be difficult if the buyer is prepared. One of the first keys is knowing *where* to look and *what* to look for once you get there. The following are some tips and reminders for the journey:

1. Do extensive research. Read books on the Rottweiler (see Useful Addresses and Literature, page 102) and learn what is acceptable for the breed. Go to dog shows and talk to breeders when they are not busy getting ready to go in the ring. Take home a catalog from the show so that those breeders whose dogs you liked can be contacted later.
2. Visit two or three kennels of breeders who impress you over the phone. Make, and then keep, an appointment with them. Breeders are always busy so you must keep your appointments and be punctual. They need to be just as impressed with you as you are with them.
3. Expect the breeder to ask as many questions of you as you do of him or her.

    Some questions the breeder may ask:

    ■ Why do you want a Rottweiler?
    ■ Have you ever owned a dog before? If so, what breed(s)?
    ■ What kinds of activities are you interested in pursuing with your dog?
    ■ How much time do you have to exercise and train the dog?
    ■ Do you have a fenced-in yard?
    ■ Where will the dog sleep?

    Answer the questions as honestly and thoroughly as possible. These answers will allow the breeder to help you choose the dog that best fits your lifestyle and expectations.

4. Look for clean, well-kept dogs and kennel areas. Some dirt is to be expected, but matted or missing fur, filthy runs and cages, rashes, or lumps are all warning signs. Think twice before you buy a dog from such a kennel. Visit more than once and try to get references.
5. Avoid buying the first puppy you see. It is always best to see more than one breeder and/or puppy for comparisons. Sometimes it does work out that you will come back to that first puppy, but make sure you have given yourself options and choices. Don't miss out on a better puppy because you are taken in by a pair of dark, brown eyes and sweet puppy breath.

Rottweilers love to lie on their backs to play and sleep.

6. Puppies need to stay with the litter for longer than six weeks. Many breeders make the mistake of letting the puppy go to a new home too early; the puppy will then miss key behavioral interactions with its littermates and mother. The ideal time to take home a puppy is when it is eight to nine weeks old.

7. If the breeder does not offer you copies of pedigrees, contracts, health certificates, and the like, ask for them. If the breeder has none of these, do *not* buy from that breeder.

What to Avoid When Choosing Your Rottweiler

1. Avoid backyard breeders. These breeders often mass-produce large numbers of pups and often sell dogs that come from substandard health conditions. They have not put thought or time into studying the best examples of the breed in order to produce mentally and physically sound dogs and have no background in showing or training the breed they sell. These puppies may have health and temperament problems.

2. Avoid the seller who does not have dogs that have been hip X-rayed and certified by the Orthopedic Foundation for Animals (OFA). Also ask about the results of the following tests performed on the parents of the puppies:

   ■ Eyes: The Canine Eye Registration Foundation (CERF) was established at Purdue University in 1974 and will provide registration for dogs found free of hereditary eye diseases. The dog must be examined by a board-certified veterinary ophthalmologist.

   ■ von Willebrand's Disease or VWD is a blood-clotting disease that is often found in Rottweilers. A blood test will diagnose VWD.

   ■ Heart tests on the sire and dam will help to ensure that the parents of your puppy are clear of subaortic stenosis (SAS).

   ■ The OFA also reads X-rays of the elbows and certifies dogs free of elbow dysplasia, a disease in which the elbow cartilage and connective tissue do not properly adjoin. This results in lameness and arthritic conditions of varying severity. It is not advisable that dogs with this condition be bred.

3. Avoid sellers who try to force a puppy on you. Good breeders want the best for their puppies and do not push you to buy a puppy.

Questions for the Breeder

■ Ask how long the breeder has been in this occupation.

■ Ask what titles his or her dogs have. Dogs that have working degrees and conformation titles have proven their ability to remain mentally and physically sound through the training required for such titles. Make sure you have done your homework regarding Obedience and Conformation titles available for dogs.

■ Ask to tour the kennels and meet the sire and dam, if possible.

- Ask for references from previous puppy buyers.
- Ask for copies of all pedigrees and contracts to take home and look over. Don't simply look at the OFA certificates; ask for copies and check them out.

Choosing the Right Puppy

Now that you found the right breeder, you have one more challenge, choosing the right puppy for you and your family. This can seem a daunting task when you are first introduced to a pack of black and tan fur balls at your breeder's home.

One of the standards for evaluating puppy personalities is the Puppy Aptitude Test or PAT. Many breeders have their pups tested professionally using this test or a version of it.

You can use the results of a PAT to help you choose the best puppy that suits your needs. Your breeder will also have invaluable information on the character and personality of each puppy.

Here are some points to remember:

1. Consider why you want the puppy. Is it to show, breed, compete in obedience or agility competitions and other dog sports?
2. Consider the amount of time you will be able to commit to training and other chores associated with dog ownership.
3. Consider your and your family members' level of exercise.
4. Consider the size of your family, whether you have small children, and most of all, make sure the whole family

The neonatal period: birth to 21 days.

agrees that it is the right time to bring home a puppy.

Even if you are not planning to show your dog in any events, the PAT will help you determine the qualities of the puppy that best suit your environment and needs. It will also help the breeder to place puppies in the correct homes.

The National Breed Club

The American Rottweiler Club (ARC) is an American Kennel Club (AKC) member club. It is recognized as the national breed club. The ARC is dedicated to education about responsible Rottweiler ownership and to preserving and protecting the Rottweiler breed (see Useful Addresses and Literature, page 102).

The socialization period: 21 to 49 days.

OFA Information

This organization examines X-rays taken by veterinarians of the dog's hips, and then rates and certifies the hips. Only hips rated *Excellent*, *Good*, or *Fair* are worthy of official certification for the dog. This nonprofit organization also supplies diagnostic services for many of the other genetic and orthopedic diseases that afflict Rottweilers including cardiac and thyroid registries and von Willebrand's Disease (see Useful Addresses and Literature, page 102).

Puppies' Developmental Stages

All dogs go through various stages of growth and development. You should be acquainted with these stages so that you will better understand what causes certain behaviors in your Rottweiler.

■ In the *neonatal period*, from birth to 21 days, not much happens in the form of learning. Pups have instincts to keep warm, find food, and eat. Behaviors are based solely on reflex and instinct. Experiments performed on pups before 21 days showed no brain wave activity when outside stimuli were applied. Sounds, scent, and sight experiments indicated no changes on the brain wave machine, and, in addition, there was hardly any difference between the waking and sleeping brain wave pattern[1].

■ The *socialization period*, from 21 days through 49 days, is a period filled with rapid physical changes and learning. The eyes open and exploration and play behaviors begin. It is extremely important that the puppy remain with its mother and littermates until after the sixth week. Even if the pups are eating on their own, their understanding of dog-to-dog etiquette is learned during the fifth and sixth weeks. They learn play, dominance and submission, bite inhibition, and other behaviors.

■ The *fear imprint period* is from 7 to 12 weeks. In this stage of development, the puppy is most susceptible to experiences that may cause fear. All experiences it has during this time can have an impact on the puppy and its future; thus, socialization with humans is important during this phase. This is the best time to bring the puppy to its new home.

■ The *flight instinct period* is between four and eight months, when the puppy goes through more rapid physical changes. This is the time when the puppy begins to test his wings and challenge the owner. He becomes more

[1]Phaffenberger, Clarence. *The New Knowledge of Dog Behavior*. NY: Howell Book House, 1986.

independent. Hard teething begins, as do hormonal changes. This is the most frustrating phase of the dog's life for both the pup and the owner. During this time, the second fear imprint period also takes place, adding to the puppy's mood swings and behavioral changes. The second fear imprint period is often most obvious, when the puppy seems frightened of many objects and people, even those that he has met or seen before.

Neutering and spaying are best done during this period. Neutering the male will limit his urges in the areas of territorial aggression and marking, as well as his lust for females. Spaying the female limits her mood swings and eliminates the mess of a twice yearly season and unwanted pregnancies. In addition, both of these surgeries prevent cancer of those areas removed.

Puppy Aptitude Test (PAT)

PAT uses a scoring system from one through six and consists of ten tests. The tests are done consecutively and in the order listed. Each test is scored separately and interpreted on its own merits. The scores are not averaged, and there are no winners or losers. The entire purpose of the test is to select the right puppy for the right home.

The 10 tests are as follows:

1. **Social Attraction:** The degree of social attraction to people, confidence, or dependence.

The fear imprint period: 7 to 12 weeks.

2. **Following:** The willingness to follow a person.
3. **Restraint:** The degree of dominant or submissive tendency and ease of handling stress in difficult situations.
4. **Social Dominance:** The degree of acceptance of social dominance by a person.
5. **Elevation:** The degree of accepting dominance while in a position of no control, such as at the veterinarian or groomer.
6. **Retrieving:** The degree of willingness to do something for you. Together with *Social Attraction* and *Following*, this is a key indicator for ease or difficulty in training.
7. **Touch Sensitivity:** The degree of sensitivity to touch. This is a key indicator to the type of training equipment required.
8. **Sound Sensitivity:** The degree of sensitivity to sound, such as loud noises or thunderstorms.

9. **Sight Sensitivity:** The degree of response to a moving object, such as chasing bicycles, children, or squirrels.
10. **Stability:** The degree of startle response to a strange object.

How to Test

The ground rules for performing the test are discussed below.

- The testing should be done in a location unfamiliar to the puppies. This does not mean they have to be taken away from home. A 10-foot square area is perfectly adequate, such as an unfamiliar room in the house.
- The puppies are tested one at a time.
- There are no other dogs or people in the testing area except for the scorer and the tester.
- The puppies do not know the tester.
- The scorer is a third party and not the person interested in selling you the puppy.
- The scorer is unobtrusive and is positioned so he or she can observe the puppies' responses without having to move.
- The puppies are tested before they are fed.

TOP DOG TIP

During testing maintain a positive, upbeat, and friendly attitude toward the puppies. Try to get each puppy to interact with you bringing out the best in him or her. Make the test a pleasant experience for the puppy.

The flight instinct period: 4 to 8 months.

- The puppies are tested when they are at their liveliest.
- Do not try to test a puppy that is not feeling well.
- Puppies should not be tested the day of or the day after being vaccinated.
- Only the first response counts!

The tests are simple to perform, and can be conducted by anyone with some common sense. If needed, you can elicit the help of someone who has experience in testing puppies.

Testing

Here is a step-by-step discussion on how each of the 10 tests will be conducted.

1. **Social Attraction:** The owner or caretaker of the puppy places it in the test area about four feet from the tester and then leaves the test area. The tester kneels down and coaxes the puppy to come to him or her by encouragingly and gently clapping hands and calling. The tester must coax the puppy in the opposite direction from where it entered the test area. Hint: Lean backward, sitting on your heels instead of leaning forward toward the puppy. Instead of trying to reach for the puppy, keep your hands close to your body and encourage the puppy to come to you.

2. **Following:** The tester stands up and slowly walks away encouraging the puppy to follow. Hint: Make sure the

puppy sees you walk away. Get the puppy to focus on you by lightly clapping your hands. Use verbal encouragement to get the puppy to follow you. Do not lean over the puppy.

3. **Restraint:** The tester crouches down and gently rolls the puppy on its back. The puppy is held on its back for 30 seconds. Hint: Hold the puppy down without applying too much pressure. The object is not to keep it on its back, but rather to test its response to being placed in that position.

4. **Social Dominance:** Let the puppy stand up or sit, and gently stroke it from the head to the back while you crouch beside it. See if it will lick your face, which is an indication of a forgiving nature. Continue stroking the puppy until you see a behavior you

An alert pup will be easier to focus during training.

can score. Hint: When you crouch next to the puppy avoid leaning or hovering over the puppy. Have the puppy at your side with both of you facing in the same direction.

5. **Elevation Dominance:** The tester cradles the puppy with both hands, supporting the puppy under its chest, and gently lifts it two feet off the ground. The puppy is held there for 30 seconds.

6. **Retrieving:** The tester crouches beside the puppy and attracts its attention with a crumpled up piece of paper. When the puppy shows some interest, the tester throws the paper no more than four feet in front of the puppy and encourages it to retrieve the paper.

7. **Touch Sensitivity:** The tester locates the webbing of one of the puppy's front paws and presses it lightly between his index finger and thumb. The tester gradually increases pressure while counting to ten and stops when the puppy pulls away or shows signs of discomfort.

8. **Sound Sensitivity:** The puppy is placed in the center of the testing area and an assistant stationed at the perimeter makes a sharp noise, such as banging a metal spoon on the bottom of a metal pan.

9. **Sight Sensitivity:** The puppy is placed in the center of the testing area. The tester ties a string around a bath towel and jerks it across the floor, two feet away from the puppy.

10. **Stability:** An umbrella is opened about five feet from the puppy and gently placed on the ground.

Scoring the Results

The table on pages 14 and 15 shows the responses you will see, and the score assigned to each particular response. You will notice some variations and will have to make a judgment on what score best applies.

What Do the Scores Mean?

The scores are interpreted as follows:

Mostly 1s

- Has a strong desire to be pack leader and is not shy about bucking for a promotion.
- Has a predisposition to be aggressive toward people and other dogs and will bite.
- Should only be placed into a very experienced home where the dog will be trained and worked on a regular basis.

Mostly 2s

- Has leadership aspirations.
- May be hard to manage and has the capacity to bite.
- Has lots of self-confidence.
- Should not be placed into an inexperienced home.

TOP DOG TIP

Stay away from the puppy with a lot of 1s or 2s. He has lots of leadership aspirations and may be difficult to manage. This puppy needs an experienced home and will not be good with children.

Puppies should show lots of interest in toys.

- Too unruly to be good with children, elderly people, or other animals.
- Needs a strict schedule, loads of exercise, and lots of training.
- Has the potential to be a great show dog when paired with someone who understands dog behavior.

Mostly 3s

- Can be a high-energy dog and may need lots of exercise.
- Good with people and other animals.
- Can be a bit of a handful to live with.
- Needs training, does very well at it, and learns quickly.
- Great dog for second time owner.

Puppy Aptitude Responses and Test Scores

Test	Response	Score
SOCIAL ATTRACTION	Came readily, tail up, jumped, bit at hands	1
	Came readily, tail up, pawed, licked at hands	2
	Came readily, tail up	3
	Came readily, tail down	4
	Came hesitantly, tail down	5
	Didn't come at all	6
FOLLOWING	Followed readily, tail up, got underfoot, bit at feet	1
	Followed readily, tail up, got underfoot	2
	Followed readily, tail up	3
	Followed readily, tail down	4
	Followed hesitantly, tail down	5
	Did not follow or went away	6
RESTRAINT	Struggled fiercely, flailed, bit	1
	Struggled fiercely, flailed	2
	Settled, struggled, settled with some eye contact	3
	Struggled, then settled	4
	No struggle	5
	No struggle, strained to avoid eye contact	6
SOCIAL DOMINANCE	Jumped, pawed, bit, growled	1
	Jumped, pawed	2
	Cuddled up to tester and tried to lick face	3
	Squirmed, licked at hands	4
	Rolled over, licked at hands	5
	Went away and stayed away	6
ELEVATION DOMINANCE	Struggled fiercely, tried to bite	1
	Struggled fiercely	2
	Struggled, settled, struggled, settled	3
	No struggle, relaxed	4
	No struggle, body stiff	5
	No struggle, froze	6

Test	Response	Score
RETRIEVING	Chased object, picked it up and ran away	1
	Chased object, stood over it and did not return	2
	Chased object, picked it up and returned with it to tester	3
	Chased object and returned without it to tester	4
	Started to chase object, lost interest	5
	Does not chase object	6
TOUCH SENSITIVITY	8–10 count before response	1
	6–8 count before response	2
	5–6 count before response	3
	3–5 count before response	4
	2–3 count before response	5
	1–2 count before response	6
SOUND SENSITIVITY	Listened, located sound, and ran toward it barking	1
	Listened, located sound, and walked slowly toward it	2
	Listened, located sound, and showed curiosity	3
	Listened and located sound	4
	Cringed, backed off, and hid behind tester	5
	Ignored sound and showed no curiosity	6
SIGHT SENSITIVITY	Looked, attacked, and bit object	1
	Looked and put feet and mouth on object	2
	Looked with curiosity and attempted to investigate, tail up	3
	Looked with curiosity, tail down	4
	Ran away or hid behind tester	5
	Hid behind tester	6
STABILITY	Looked and ran to the umbrella, mouthing or biting it	1
	Looked and walked to the umbrella, smelling it cautiously	2
	Looked and went to investigate	3
	Sat and looked, but did not move toward the umbrella	4
	Showed little or no interest	5
	Ran away from the umbrella	6

Mostly 4s

- The kind of dog that makes the perfect pet.
- Best choice for the first time owner.
- Rarely will buck for a promotion in the family.
- Easy to train and rather quiet.
- Good with elderly people and children; although, he may need protection from the children.
- Choose this puppy. Take it to obedience classes, and you'll be the star without having to do too much work!

Mostly 5s

- Fearful, shy, and needs special handling.
- Will run away at the slightest stress in its life.
- Strange people, strange places, different floor or ground surfaces may upset it.
- Often afraid of loud noises and terrified of thunderstorms. When you greet it upon your return, may submissively urinate. Needs a very special home where the environment doesn't change too much, and where there are no children.
- Best for a quiet, elderly couple.
- If cornered and cannot get away, has a tendency to bite.

Mostly 6s

- So independent that he doesn't need you or other people.
- Doesn't care if he is trained or not—he is his own person. Unlikely to bond with you, since he doesn't need you.
- A great guard dog for gas stations!
- Do not take this puppy thinking you can change him into a lovable bundle. You can't! Leave well enough alone.

Interpreting the Scores

Few puppies will test with all 2s or all 3s—there will be a mixture of scores. For that first time, wonderfully easy to train, potential star, look for a puppy that scores with mostly 4s and 3s. Don't worry about the score on Touch Sensitivity, you can compensate for that with the right training equipment.

Avoid the puppy with a score of one on the Restraint and Elevation tests. This puppy will be too much for the first time owner.

It's a lot more fun to have a good dog, one that is easy to train, one you can live with, and one you can be proud of, than one that is a constant struggle. *(Copyright 2007–2008 Jack and Wendy Volhard. www.volhard.com)*

3 *Starting the Training Program*

The Importance of a Social Life

Nothing else can prepare your puppy for the rigors of his future as socializing with other puppies and people. Besides socializing with other animals, it is important that the pup experience different sights and sounds and meet different types of people every day. Keeping Fritz from the world can make him shy and fearful, which can cause him to begin biting at or lunging toward the object of his fear. The inherent danger of this sort of behavior is obvious. With that in mind, the following steps are advised:

1. Begin socializing Fritz from the day he comes home. Be careful to limit his outings until he has visited the veterinarian and has had at least two rounds of vaccinations that include inoculations against Bordatella and Parvovirus. Try inviting neighbors or friends to your house instead of taking Fritz out until these vaccinations are completed.
2. Limit visits to once a day and just one or two people at first. Let Fritz see and hear their voices, play a little, and then go to his crate. This will teach him to accept visitors, get a little attention, and then mind his business elsewhere.
3. Once his vaccinations are underway, Fritz can begin full socializing. This means taking him for short walks in the park and your neighborhood, on lead, of course. Though he may seem to want to stay close to you, it takes only a second for him to run off; therefore, safeguard your puppy whenever you take him out by keeping him on leash. Every time someone wants to greet your puppy, tell him to *"Say hello,"* then allow the person to come up to him. It is often helpful to have that person kneel down to the puppy at first.
4. Help Fritz by holding him loosely by the lead, and keeping your hand at the base of his tail as you hold him in a *sit* position. Young pups are too excited to remember to stay or sit on command. Sometimes it is even helpful to use the other hand at the base of the puppy's chest to keep him still. It is much more successful for everyone to concentrate on the greeting at this point, rather than the obedience commands themselves.
5. Whenever Fritz is out in the world, meeting people and other animals, he is

experiencing *socialization*; however, it is important that the encounters be positive or you will risk harming his outlook on new situations. Avoid overstimulation by keeping walks and visits short.

6. Watch carefully for signs of stress. These include hiding, panting, drooling, and sweating from the paw pads. If Fritz seems afraid of something, don't force him toward the object or person. Keep the lead loose and approach the object. Smile and touch the object and kneel down next to it. If he is still reluctant after a minute or so, simply stop and move on. Try the same object or person a little later, if you can.

7. Another good source of stimulation and socialization is a puppy preschool class. These classes are offered by many dog trainers and are the key to a well-rounded puppy. It is extremely important that the trainer you choose knows about puppy development and training. In addition, the instructors need wide experience in all breeds of dogs, Rottweilers included. If the instructor shows hesitation or fear of the Rottweiler, look for another. A good facility will take care to demand and check on all vaccinations of the dogs attending the school. Indoor facilities are best, especially for puppies, as they are easier to clean and disinfect. In addition, puppies can be safely let off leash

---

TOP DOG TIP

See Chapter 5 for instruction on leash and collar training and teaching the puppy his name.

---

for socialization time. After finding a good preschool for your pup, let the fun begin!

Children and Rottweilers

As with any other breed of dog, it is important to socialize the Rottweiler to children.

Most working breeds are prey-oriented. Breeds such as the Rottweiler often have extremely high *prey drive*; watching children run and play can activate the need within the dog to chase prey.

Rottweiler pups need to be around children of all ages. Even if the household the Rottweiler lives in does not have children living there, it is still an important part of training; after all, children are everywhere. They make strange sounds and they move quickly. If Mollie is not used to seeing and hearing children as they play, she may be more likely to chase a child as prey. One way you can help your Rottweiler become used to children is to take walks in parks. Let Mollie see and hear the sounds and actions of children playing on at least a weekly basis.

Whenever your Rottweiler shows calm, quiet behavior around or near children, praise her. Any time she sits and greets a child quietly, praise her and feed her a treat. If she does get overexcited, remain calm. Take her *scruff* firmly and calmly tell her *"Sit."* Hold her until she is calm again, then repeat the greeting routine.

It is not wise to leave children of any age alone with any dog, as play can get out of hand. Even the most docile of Rottweilers may become agitated if a child inadvertently pokes an eye or steps on a paw.

Respect from Children

Children also need to learn to respect dogs. The best way to teach this is to make sure all children coming in contact with Mollie understand the rules:

- No running and screaming.
- No hitting or kicking the dog.
- Mollie's crate or bed is the one area where she can go to rest and get away from stress. Do not allow children to play in or around the crate.

Daily Handling

Your children and your Rottweiler will also benefit from daily handling sessions with the puppy. Touching and grooming is the best way to start. Touch Mollie and feed a treat. Praise her with *"Good dog,"* then have the child do the same.

Children often tend to snatch their hands away and up, which causes the puppy to follow the movement. This causes jumping up and nipping behaviors. Emphasize the importance of moving the hands slowly and firmly, not rapidly.

Neighborhood Children

Even the neighborhood children benefit from being introduced to a new Rottweiler puppy when it first comes home. Letting

It is important to socialize the Rottweiler to children.

TOP DOG TIP

If the child is carrying something, such as food or books, teach the child to throw it off to the side, away from the dog, and away from the direction in which the child needs to go. Dogs that want to attack are often highly prey-oriented and will chase the item, which may give the child a chance to move off slowly in the other direction while the dog investigates. Remember, teach your child to throw away from the dog, not toward the dog.

them in on the care and training of the dog will also help them to treat the dog with respect. Invite parents to come over and greet Mollie with their children; for example, discuss how the children can get involved by going on walks with you and the puppy. To avoid a parade every time you go for a walk with Mollie, make sure that children and parents realize you will invite them when it is convenient for you to include them on a walk.

Children can also play the recall game (see Chapter 7) with the new puppy. This game teaches the puppy that children are allowed to give commands that she must follow. It also teaches children to remain still around her and let her come to them.

Safety Measures to Take to Prevent Bites

All children should know what to do in the event of a dog attack. Practicing what to do and how to behave around any dog can prevent accidents and tragedies.

Make the crate a safe haven for the puppy.

Keep things simple and fun so your child will revert to safety measures automatically. (These rules apply to any age person who encounters dogs.)

1. Never approach or pet any strange dog, even if the dog belongs to a neighbor. Always ask to pet someone's dog first; never run up to a dog and start petting.
2. Never tease dogs.
3. If you see a strange dog coming toward you, do not run or scream; instead, turn your head and look away, fold your arms in front of your body, and try to go off in a different direction at a normal walk.
4. If a dog is coming toward you, look for *up* signs—tail, lips, hair, and ears. If any are up, the dog may attack. If the *up* signs are there, freeze. Freezing consists of turning the head away from the dog, and folding the arms in front of the body. Do not move or make any noise. When the dog moves off, do not go on too quickly. Keep your motions as calm and as normal as possible.
5. Tell your child to come immediately home after any episode with a dog and tell you where the dog was and exactly what happened. Try to get information on the color and other characteristics of the dog.

Rottweilers generally love children as long as they are properly introduced to them. It is up to owners to make sure that any youngster is safe around the dog they own. More information on *desensitization* and handling is found in Chapter 4.

4 Learning to Teach and Making It Fun

Operant Conditioning and How It Aids Training

The training in this book is based on the science of *operant conditioning*, a method of training that is based on the observation that responses rewarded positively are more quickly repeated in the future. Conversely, behaviors *not* rewarded or even *ignored* are less likely to be repeated.

A Marker Word

Positive *reinforcement* is different from praise; it is delivered during the behavior that the handler wishes to have repeated and, in order for it to work, a *marker* word or sound must be taught.

The handler must use the word *"Yes"* each time the dog does something correctly on his own, the first time you tell him. This is operant conditioning. Simple and painless? Well, there are some rules surrounding the use of this method.

First, deliver the *"Yes"* marker at the moment you see the desired behavior and say it only once. It is important to use the same tone and inflection each time you use this marker. When first training a new behavior, make sure you follow the marker with the positive reinforcement— probably a treat. A favored toy will also work, but the timing must be exact and the dog needs to be allowed to have the toy for a few moments in order for it to become a true positive reinforcer.

The *conditioned reinforcement* (CR) or marker is introduced as follows:

Step A. Gather Fritz and a pile of treats. Hold one treat in your right hand, preferably closed in your fist. A leash is optional. If Fritz is on lead, keep it loose; in fact, stand on it.

Step B. Extend your left hand toward Fritz. Make it obvious that he should look at or touch that hand. Most dogs will sniff the hand. Immediately say *"Yes."* Give the treat from the right hand. Continue to do this until Fritz is indicating the left hand emphatically.

TOP DOG TIP

Try not to speak to the dog; just smile a lot and let the dog do the thinking.

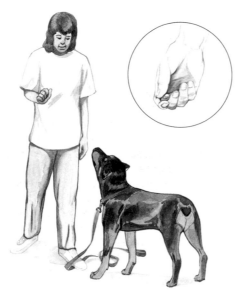

Hold a treat in your closed right hand.

> ## TOP DOG TIP
> These sessions can last up to five minutes at a time. Stop before the dog loses interest; it is best to have a session when he is hungry.

Encourage the dog to look at or touch the left hand.

Feed with the right hand just after you mark the behavior.

Gradually teach the dog to move in all directions.

Step C. Begin moving the left hand further away from Fritz's face in different directions. Move it slightly to your left several inches. If he does not seem interested, wiggle your fingers. As soon as he shows interest in the hand or touches the hand, say *"Yes."*

Step D. Practice two or three times a day. Try to accomplish the following:

- The dog will get up and move toward the left hand in order to touch it.

- The dog will turn his head to the left or right to follow the hand.
- The dog will jump up slightly to reach the hand.
- The dog will bring his head toward the floor to touch the hand.

Step E. Begin to have Fritz move from one area to another, watching your hand. Step backward and have him follow the left hand; move forward or move your hand in a slow semicircle to your left so that he winds up next to your left side.

The dog brings his head down toward the hand.

More Hints

As you train, gradually increase the time Fritz must continue the behavior you are asking for before giving the marker and treat. Begin to randomize the treat; if he is given a treat for everything, it is no longer special. However, keep in mind that stopping the treat reinforcement altogether will also cause you to lose the behaviors you have taught.

Remember, you are not using operant conditioning correctly if you use the food to lure the behavior and then feed the dog the lure. Instead, he needs to learn that the food is a result of a correctly delivered behavior and does not necessarily have to be visible in order for him to receive it.

Putting this concept in terms we can understand will help. Think about jobs and paychecks. You do not see your pay or paycheck every day, yet you know you will receive it; therefore, you continue to do your job, knowing the pay will arrive. Bonus money or recognition from the employer for a specific task done particularly well makes you more likely to repeat that task on a regular basis in the hope of receiving the coveted reinforcement.

The Clicker

A clicker is much like the dime store toys of old or the counters that bankers used to use. Modern-day training clickers are generally made of plastic and house a thin piece of metal. When the piece of metal on the outside is pushed downward, it clicks on the inside piece, making a sharp, clear, noise. Clickers serve the

Desensitization acclimates a puppy to being touched.

same purpose as the word *"Yes."* They are highly recommended for use in training because they deliver the same sound in the same way each time.

Daily Training Moments

Your Rottweiler is always learning something, so it is important to provide positive learning opportunities. Throughout the day, there are always occasions for teaching. These occasions need not be time-consuming or complicated; in fact, the simpler and quicker they are, the more the dog enjoys learning.

Continue using food to enhance learning. Dogs of any age will comprehend lessons much faster when motivated by something they want. In the case of

Rottweilers, food is likely to be a great inducement.

Sit

One of the best times to teach Fritz is just before mealtime. Since most dogs eat twice a day, use a few pieces of the food to teach something each time he is fed. For instance, teaching the *sit* is as easy as holding a treat in your hand at the dog's nose. Tip your hand back slowly and Fritz will follow it with his head. His bottom will naturally hit the floor. As he begins to sit, say *"Sit,"* and immediately deliver the piece of food when he is in a full *sit.* Praise vocally with *"Good dog."* Do this three or four times during each meal preparation.

Desensitization

Another quick exercise that involves handling. Hold a piece of food at Fritz's nose with one hand and grasp his collar with the other. Praise him and feed him the piece of food, or try picking up his foot or ear for variety. This is called *desensitization* and is a wonderful way to teach a puppy to accept all sorts of touching and handling.

Attention Training

Begin teaching Fritz his name as well as attention training by using a piece of food. Say his name and a command such as *"Look."* Hold the piece of food near your waist in your left hand and smile. When he looks up, say *"Yes,"* praise, and feed a treat from your right hand. Practice holding his attention for gradually longer periods before feeding. Never give the food if the dog isn't looking. Learn more about attention training in Chapter 7.

Shaping Behavior

Naptimes are a good time for *shaping* behavior, especially for a puppy. When the puppy is tired, practice handling exercises. Brief periods of brushing, combing, and handling the feet and ears are a good way to start. Use small bits of treat to reinforce good behavior.

Handling and Submission Exercises

You can also practice *submission* exercises that will help the puppy learn to be handled without resisting. They teach acceptance of leadership as well as self-control during restraint. Self-control is important for any dog to learn.

The exercises discussed here are all ways of immediately taking control of your new puppy. They are ways of transferring him from his old pack—his mother and littermates—to his new one—you and your family. Performed daily, they will accustom the puppy to your calm leadership ability.

These exercises include *cradling* the puppy upside down in your arms. Smile and talk to him softly while doing this. If he struggles, remain calm and hold him firmly. Stop talking. When he quiets, praise him softly and continue holding

Teach your Rottweiler to accept having his feet handled.

him a few more seconds. If he remains calm, praise him softly and release. Gradually increase the time you expect him to be calm (about a minute is a good goal).

Sitting on the Floor with Your Puppy

You can also sit on the floor with Fritz between your stretched-out legs. Gently turn him on his back and support him with your legs, his head in your lap. Rub his tummy, but if he struggles, freeze and hold him firmly. Use your legs to keep him from escaping. Say nothing. When he quiets and calms, resume rubbing him gently and talking softly. Release the puppy only when he is quiet and calm.

These exercises help the puppy learn to be submissive without violence on your part or on his part. Remain calm and quiet during these exercises. If you become upset, the puppy will become more upset. If he is allowed to get up when he struggles, then he is learning that struggling, growling, or biting is the key to avoiding

restraint. Be firm in your decision to be the leader from the start and avoid having a Rottweiler that bosses you around.

The Muzzle Hold

Another handling exercise that will help your puppy calm down and stop barking or biting is a simple muzzle hold. Encircle the muzzle around the area just below

Even larger, older dogs should accept being held gently in any position.

Fritz's eyes (the stop) with your thumb and forefinger. Gently hold while saying *"Quiet"* or *"Stop."* The second he stops, praise him, and release the muzzle. When holding the muzzle, it is important not to grab or squeeze or cover the puppy's nostrils; it is the positioning of the hold that matters in relaying your intent.

The muzzle hold works by using the pup's natural instincts. It is frequently used by older, superior dogs when chastising exuberant pups and younger dogs. The older dog will hold the muzzle closed using his mouth over the pup's muzzle. It firmly tells the offender to calm down, be quiet, or stop that. The uses of this muzzle hold can also help to lay the groundwork for control in the *walk*. The head collar training systems work by using the same premise to prevent and control lunging and aggression on lead. (Read more on training collars in Chapter 5.)

The Scruff

A final exercise in handling is to lay Fritz gently on his side with his feet facing away from you. Gather the skin at the back of his neck in the hand that is closest to that area. This is the scruff. Hold it firmly, but do not squeeze. Rest your other hand on his back, upper leg, or hip area. Tell him *"Settle."* Be calm and quiet. Hold him flat on his side. If he is calm, praise him softly but not frequently.

The muzzle hold communicates calm control to the dog.

If he struggles, hold on and say nothing. As soon as he is calm and quiet, praise him again and release him. Practice this exercise daily for a week or two. Make sure you have 10 or 15 minutes to work with the puppy. Five minutes is a good start; gradually work up to a longer and longer period of settling the puppy.

Eventually, Fritz will begin calming whenever you say the word *"Settle"* or take his scruff. When you see this begin to happen, you know he is accepting your leadership. It can take many weeks of practice. As you see him begin to understand, start using the command or taking the scruff whenever you see him getting out of control. It will be his cue to calm down.

Playing

Playing is also a wonderful way to teach your Rottweiler. There are different games you can teach him to play that will also educate him in the area of leadership and obedience. These games will be covered in Chapters 6 and 7.

Leadership: The Key to Success

Much has been written about leadership. Many handlers, owners, and trainers assume that more is better in convincing the Rottweiler who is boss; however, the use of violence does nothing to teach leadership. Hitting, kicking, slapping, and screaming at the dog serve no purpose in the long run and often lead to more violence—on the part of the dog.

A firm grip on the scruff is used during the *settle*.

The most important thing to remember is that *fear is not respect*. Rottweilers can become violent or fearful when confronted. Either reaction is incorrect, unnecessary, and, of course, dangerous. Teaching through leadership is more humane, and fun for both you and the dog.

The *settle* exercise helps calm and control the dog.

What Is Leadership?

Leadership is an important part of the Rottweiler's character. If your dog does not think anyone in the household is the leader, then your dog will make it his business to become the leader.

To understand the subtle differences between dominance and leadership, one must have a clear understanding of how dogs behave and deal with one another. The drives of the dog include *pack drive*. Packs must have a leader. If there is no leader, then it's not a pack. The dog in charge gains the leadership position by demonstrating his skills to all the others. He is accepted by all the others until someone comes along and demonstrates that he or she has better skills.

Some of this involves what humans would consider violent behavior, but is actually acceptable to a dog; for instance, one dog will hold down the other dog. You can use the same teaching method by using the submission exercises described earlier in this chapter. Ideally, the owner is quietly in charge, demonstrates fairness, and stands his or her ground using body language. This change in attitude toward the dog is more successful than using violence.

If you see Fritz doing something he shouldn't, use a sharp (not loud), clipped sound such as *"Hey, hey,"* and stand up quickly with your upper body moving forward. Put a frown on your face. Most pups will be startled and jump away. Immediately relax your body, smile, and praise Fritz if he has stopped the behavior. Redirect him to a proper form of entertainment such as chewing a toy, and praise again.

In the dog/owner relationship, you should always be the leader. The confidence the dog gains in you through this perception of you as leader translates into teamwork. This is what your relationship with your Rottweiler is all about.

Pack Drive

Pack drive is an example of why teamwork is so important—the pack must work together to survive. The pack must have confidence that each member of the pack whether two or six—can do its share of the work, will not let the others down, and will follow orders. That is how mistakes are kept to a minimum. If one member fails, the others are all likely to go hungry. This is why leadership is taught first, then simple obedience, followed by more precise work. The dog must first understand who is running the show in order to be a working part of the show.

Puppies learn leadership quickly through the early training and socialization covered in this chapter, but older dogs can also be taught. As a matter of course, your Rottweiler needs to recognize your leadership before real obedience exercises begin. Once he accepts your touch and reacts to restraint in a calm manner, you are well on the way to having a learning partner and companion.

5 *Training Tools*

There are a number of different tools to use to train your Rottweiler; using a variety of tools will give better training results. The tools found in this section will improve control and communication with your Rottie.

Leash and Collar

It is important to use a leash and collar with your Rottweiler from the first day in your home. It is much safer for a dog to always be on lead. Also, if the dog can move away from you, you cannot follow through with the commands you are teaching. If this happens just a few times, the dog will quickly learn to ignore you (see Collar and Leash Training, page 37).

Sizes and Styles of Leashes

There are various lengths and styles of leashes. The regular training leash should be about 6 to 8 feet (1.8 to 2.4 m) long. It can be leather, nylon, or other material, but make sure it is comfortable in your hand. Use a fairly wide leash approximately 1/2 inch to 1 inch (1.25 to 2.5 cm) wide or more. A stout leash will give more support when you need to use some

muscle with your Rottweiler—using a thin leash is like trying to walk an elephant with a strand of spaghetti. Most obedience classes use the 6-foot (1.8-m) lead for early training. It keeps the handler close to the dog, allowing the handler to follow through with commands more quickly.

Flexi-Lead: Once the training is understood by the dog, you will want to allow him more freedom on walks, while still having control. At that time, try another leash called the *Flexi-Lead*. This is a long, retractable line encased in a plastic holder with a handle. The outgoing line can be stopped with a button in an instant. The line retracts automatically, eliminating the dangerous tangling that often occurs with a regular long line.

A Flexi-Lead is helpful in allowing the dog to get more exercise on long walks while still being safe on a lead. It is also a wonderful training tool when the dog is at a point where you are adding some distance to exercises such as the *come-when-called* and the *stay* exercises.

Collars

There are a number of different collars to train with, but the one I recommend the most often is a plain leather or nylon flat

Walking on a Flexi-Lead.

fort. When you examine the handling exercises that teach your dog to accept control, you will see that these collars are a breakthrough in training.

Head collars will firmly control the dog by turning his head each time he pulls on the leash; thus, the handler does not have to jerk or pull hard to control the dog. I recommend this type of collar for all dogs that pull or lunge. In addition, it often has a calming effect on aggression; because there is no discomfort involved for the dog, frustration is diminished. This helps the handler stay calm, which is imperative in situations that involve aggression. The head collar system is also a perfect addition to the positive motivation methods discussed here.

In Chapter 6 you will learn how the head collar looks and works on the Rottweiler.

buckle collar. If motivation and leadership methods are started early, you may never need another collar.

The newest training collars, head collars, are readily recommended by an increasing number of trainers, veterinarians, and behaviorists across the country. These collars are known as Gentle Leaders and Haltis. They work using the same instincts the dog understands regarding control. While the two collars listed here are different in some ways, the basic premise is the same: The collars gently yet firmly control the head at two points— the muzzle and the back of the neck.

Many pet dog trainers are using head collar systems instead of choke and prong collars, because they are less harsh and do not choke the dog or cause him discom-

The Gentle Leader head collar helps keep the dog from pulling on the leash.

Toys

Using a favorite toy for training is a great advantage; most Rottweilers love to chase a ball or other toy. They love to play tug-o-war. The key to using toys as training tools is to keep a variety on hand and only bring them out when you are training. Make the toy special by only interacting with it when the dog is interacting with you. This motivates the dog to want to work and earn that toy.

When Fritz performs an exercise well, pull the toy out of a pocket and throw it to him. Or, have him play tug-enough (see page 42). Let him play for a few seconds and then go back to work. Soon, he will eagerly perform the exercises in order to earn the favored toy.

If at any time Fritz does not seem interested in working, make a big deal out of ending the whole session. Stop everything, put away the toy, and put him in the house or kennel. This tells him that training time and fun will end if his attention drifts.

In order to keep Fritz interested and his motivation high, try to end each session while he is still slightly energetic and wants to play. This will encourage his interest the next time the special toys come out.

Use a toy to reward the dog during training.

buying successful toys that keep your dog busy. The Rottweiler puppy or dog needs stimulation and fun in order to preserve your household and its contents. Having a variety of interesting, tasty, and safe toys will help keep your Rottie busy and

Types of Toys

While stocking up on training toys is important, it is also important to have toys that keep your dog happy when you are *not* training. Remember that buying many toys does not take the place of

Playing tug games is a favorite reward for many Rottweilers.

Successful toys are those that the puppy enjoys . . .

so she won't use your shoes as toys!

happy. The following plastic and rubber toys can be placed in the dishwasher for cleaning. The fleecy toys and tugs should be washed in the washing machine.

- **Stuffed Bones:** Various sizes of hollow bones that are stuffed with dried liver, bits of dog food, or other small treats are the number one home-alone toys for many owners and their dogs. These hard bones will keep Fritz occupied for long periods, and will help keep him occupied in his crate or when you just want him to settle down for a while in the house (for more on stuffed bones and chewing, see page 44).
- **Synthetic Bones:** These are hard plastic bones that come in various shapes and sizes. They may also have flavors added, such as ham or peanut butter.
- **Kong Toys:** Hard rubber toys, also known as Tuffies, are available. They are shaped like cones, and are hollow inside. Use pieces of biscuits to stuff inside them. The dog bats them, bounces them around, and is rewarded with pieces falling out.
- **Extreme Goody Balls and Spaceships:** These are hard rubber toys with "goodie grabbers" that firmly hold the pieces of treat inside, making the reward of pulling out a piece a little harder to accomplish.
- **Buster Cubes and Treat Balls:** These are hard plastic cubes or balls that dispense treats randomly as they are pushed by the dog. Place a handful of dog food inside them. They are

best used outdoors or in large rooms. They keep dogs active and busy.

- **Fleecy Toys:** Fleecy toys come in all shapes and sizes. They can be used for tug-o-war games during play and training and to teach the tug-enough game (see page 42). These toys are not recommended for long periods of unsupervised play. They can be washed in the washing machine and put in the dryer.

- **Chewmen:** These are fleecy toys that are also stuffed and have squeakers. They are also good for tug games and supervised play, and are machine washable and dryable. Make sure you keep close track of toys that have squeakers; don't leave your dog alone with such toys, or he may try to eat the squeaker and could choke.

Most pet stores carry these toys and all kinds of treats and biscuits to stuff them with. There are various sizes and brands to choose from. Be sure to keep in mind the size of your Rottweiler, and buy accordingly. Small toys will be destroyed quickly and pose choking hazards for large breeds. Keep an eye on all your dog's toys for cracks, chips, breakage,

and tearing. Remove and replace these toys. Experiment with different brands for optimal results.

Treats

Another valuable motivation for the dog is food. Many people resist using treats in training because they think the dog will do the exercises only for food. This is untrue, as long as the food is used wisely and correctly.

Food is not used as a bribe; it is used to help the dog understand which behaviors

---

TOP DOG TIP

When using treats and biscuits for training sessions and for stuffing toys, keep in mind that your dog is eating extra calories. It is advisable that you cut back on your dog's daily ration of dog food when using the methods in this book. This will not only keep your dog from gaining extra weight, but will increase his appetite for training bits and keep him working for the hidden treats in bones and toys.

A variety of tug and play toys (from left to right): rope/fleecy doll; booda rope; long, fleecy tug with squeaker; soft ball; round, fleecy tug without squeaker.

A variety of toys will keep your Rottweiler busy.

ing the correct behavior. Humans often forget that dogs cannot link consequences to behavior that is in the past. For instance, when we call a dog to us and then apply a negative, the dog associates *come-when-called* with that negative.

A negative reinforcement is as simple as being called and immediately put in the house, or getting called and receiving medicine or a bath. If you call Fritz and physically punish him when he gets there, he will associate coming to you with punishment. This is the kind of reinforcement that quickly teaches a dog to turn tail and run when you call.

Instead, make sure Fritz immediately knows what he did right by using the word *"Yes,"* or by praising as soon as the correct behavior is offered. Conversely, make sure he knows what he did wrong as soon as the behavior starts. For instance, if he looks at the garbage can and heads toward it, clap your hands sharply and say *"Ah, ah."* This helps the dog understand immediately that you disapprove of his going into the garbage.

you like best. For instance, when Fritz sits when told, immediately say *"Yes"* and feed him a treat. Then praise vocally with *"Good dog."*

Keep the treats in your pockets, not in plain sight, so that the dog learns that the treat does not have to be in his sight in order for him to receive it; instead, he need only offer you certain behaviors on command and he will earn his reinforcement. For more on the correct use of food in training read the Operant Conditioning discussion in Chapter 4.

Timing

Dog training success is grounded in timing; it is important that you time praise and reinforcement correctly. Dogs have only a short span of a few seconds to receive reinforcement before it is too late.

It is also important, through timing, to make sure you are praising and reinforc-

Talking

Your voice is a wonderful training tool. It can encourage and praise, excite, demand, and even chastise. Used correctly, it makes a big difference during training; used incorrectly, it is detrimental to training.

Dogs react to the tone of voice. When you smile and speak excitedly, it makes the dog happy, so use a happy, excited voice when you want your dog to move

A rope toy is good for solitary play or tug games.

with or toward you. Also, use the dog's name. Heeling, walking, and coming when called are good examples of times to use a happy, excited tone of voice.

When you want Fritz to stay or be calm, it is important that your voice reflects that. Keep your tone of voice pleasant but firm. Don't use his name. If he is overexcited, slow your speech and actions. Calmly tell him what to do and help him do it, if necessary. If you are angry with him, frown and act disgusted. This will be reflected in your tone. Yelling or screaming at the dog will only frighten him.

Conversely, if you talk too much, Fritz will not be able to think, or he may decide that you are there to continually remind him of what to do and he won't try as hard to remember commands. Repeating commands such as *"Stay"* or *"Sit"* does nothing to teach the dog. Let the dog think things through. Talking or pleading during an exercise will confuse him and often cause him to stop trying.

Tug-O-War

As mentioned earlier, tug-o-war is a favorite game of many Rottweilers. This game is valuable in many ways when training and for leadership. For instance, use the tug-o-war during training sessions to reward good behavior. The key to this game is that the dog learns to let go of the toy when told. It is not a test of wills, but a reward for good training.

Played correctly, tug-o-war games will not make your dog aggressive; in fact, they can be the perfect outlet to prevent the buildup of energy that often results in aggressive behaviors.

Tug toys are usually made of fleece or rope. Find toys that are small enough to stuff in a pocket or the waistband of your pants. This way, the toy is right there to present as a reward for a job well done. Learn more about how to teach one type of this game correctly on page 42, Tug-Enough Game.

6 *First Lessons and Handling Problems*

No matter what the age of a Rottweiler, problems with behavior are bound to occur.

Puppy and adolescent dog behaviors are among the most frustrating to deal with. Add to that the size and power of the Rottweiler, and there can be disaster waiting around almost every corner.

New owners often try to teach the new member of the family everything they want him to know in just a few weeks; however, the majority of the lessons learned have nothing to do with obedience exercises. Instead, the puppy will benefit most from learning simple household rules.

These normal problems and early lessons are easily managed with good preparation and research. Work on them every day for short periods and the puppy will soon adjust to life in the household.

TOP DOG TIP

It is helpful to use a name that is short and easy to say—one or two syllables—and one that does not sound like a command word.

Teaching the Name

Whether you are bringing home a new puppy or an older dog, the first thing you will want to do is begin teaching the new member of the family his name. This can be accomplished fairly quickly. Simply put, associate the dog's name with good things and do it frequently.

Feeding time is a perfect time to use the dog's name often and positively. For example, let's call our new puppy Fritz. As you begin preparing his food, call to him, *"Fritz, time to eat!"* When he comes in to watch, say *"Hi, Fritz,"* and feed him a piece of the food. Do this a few times. Carry the bowl a few paces, and invite the dog to come along: *"Come on, Fritz."* Set the food down and say *"Fritz, here's your food."*

Use the name in conjunction with fun things—playtime, walks, and so on. Try not to use the name with negatives, especially at first. If Fritz is getting into trouble, simply use a sound to distract him and get his attention: *"Ah ah,"* or *"Hey, hey."* Within a few days, Fritz will be responding to his name on a regular basis.

Collar and Leash Training

As discussed in the preceding chapter, new puppies will need to wear a collar and walk on leash. This can be accomplished with a minimum of effort. Breeders will often begin this work for you by using puppy collars of different colors to identify puppies in the litter; therefore, many pups are already used to the feeling of something around their neck. If this is not the case with your particular puppy, then proceed with collar conditioning as soon as the puppy comes home.

Purchase a lightweight nylon collar with either a metal buckle or a quick-release clasp. Make sure it fits your puppy by putting on the collar and keeping one or two fingers under the collar as you tighten the buckle. When the collar tightens on your finger, it will be about right on your puppy.

The best time to put the collar on the puppy for the first time is when he is tired and hungry. You can then feed him to get his mind off the collar and he probably will fall asleep once he eats. He will then wake up and not notice the collar so much because it has been on him for a while. More than likely, he will scratch at it a bit, but this will not last long. Ignore any attempts at manipulation on the pup's part; he will accept his collar quickly.

Leash Conditioning

Teach Fritz to accept his leash in a few days by consistently clipping it to the collar and following him around the house

Puppy behaviors are frustrating!

or yard for a few minutes. You can even let him drag it around the house as long as you are there to untangle it and keep an eye on any chewing he might try.

Frequently take the handle end of the leash and kneel down, calling Fritz to you. Have a treat or toy ready and praise him as soon as he starts toward you. If he stops, give a tiny tug and release on the leash, and move backward immediately. He will feel the tug, but he will be quickly distracted by your movement backward. Use the toy to keep him focused on you,

---

TOP DOG TIP

Keep a careful watch on the collar's fit. Puppies grow fast and the collar will become too tight quickly. Check the collar every few days. Save the collars he outgrows and donate them to Rottweiler Rescue or to a shelter.

not on the leash. When he gets to you, play for a few seconds, feed a treat, and try again.

With daily short sessions, your puppy will begin seeing wearing the leash as a time when he gets attention and play from you. When you walk with him, don't overdo it. Puppies tire quickly and will begin to drag on the leash. Keep walks short and upbeat.

Crate-Training

New owners are especially reluctant to use a crate to house-train a puppy, but there is actually no better way to quickly house-train a dog of any age. In addition, keeping a puppy in a crate when no one is around to keep tabs on him saves rugs, furniture, shoes, and even the dog. There is no end to the trouble a bored, rambunctious puppy can find when left alone; unfortunately, that trouble could be fatal if the dog swallows something it shouldn't. Training a puppy to stay in the crate is actually a fairly easy prospect, but patience is a must.

Aside from the obvious help in house-training the new puppy, crates also provide a safe haven for him and, if introduced correctly, most dogs enjoy and use their crates regularly. They will look at them as a place to get away and to sleep in peace. Children should know that the crate is the puppy's room and that it is off-limits. Crates are also indispensable for injured or sick dogs, to keep them quiet and resting. A resting Rottweiler is less likely to pull stitches or reinjure a pulled muscle, for instance.

Conversely, do not leave a puppy for countless hours without a break. Check on him often or have someone give him a break midday. Remember to remove the collar when putting the puppy in the crate, as collars do come off and puppies will chew on or eat them. This will cause choking, stomach disorders, or blockage.

Fold-down wire crates are portable and well ventilated.

What Kind of Crate?

The type of crate you use is up to you; however, wire crates provide more air circulation. Also, using a fold-down suitcase-style crate makes it easier for you to move it. Put the crate in the area of the house where most of the family congregates, such as the living room or den when the family is watching TV, and the bedroom at night.

Another type of crate is called the Vari-Kennel, more commonly known as a shipping crate. This is a fiberglass crate with grating in the door and vent grates at the top. These crates work well but they are bulky and do not fold for transporting.

Bedding in the Crate

The preferred type of bedding in a puppy crate is old towels or a blanket. These can be washed easily and are inexpensive. Most pups will chew on them, so keep an eye out for chewing and remove fraying bedding, replacing it with new. Other bedding for older dogs includes fleece kennel liners or foam mats covered with a washable material.

Many dogs prefer no bedding in their crate, since it is cooler for them to lie on the metal pan in the bottom. Some of the newer crates have a hard plastic pan in the bottom as well, and many dogs do not mind lying on this. No matter what bedding you choose, however, make sure the dog is not chewing on it and eating pieces. If he is, remove the bedding immediately to prevent the dog from getting sick. Replace it with something else or leave no bedding at all in the crate.

The Vari-Kennel is good for traveling.

Crate-Training Puppies

From the moment the puppy comes home, the crate is his place. Feed him his meals in the crate, and put the crate near your bed at night so he will feel less alone. Yes, the puppy will cry the first few nights. To help stop crying behavior quickly, take the following steps:

1. Never let the puppy out of the crate when he is howling or crying; wait for even a few seconds of quiet before you open the door. Once Fritz realizes he can get out if he hollers, he becomes a champion at crying the moment you place him in the crate.
2. Make sure the puppy has an evening playtime so he is more likely to settle down and go to sleep quickly.

Use old towels or a blanket for bedding.

3. Limit the pup's water intake during the evening; usually after 7 P.M. is good. If the puppy seems to need water, give him a few ice cubes to chew. Always take him outside one last time before crating him for the night.

4. During the pup's first week home, it is often better to get up quietly with him in the middle of the night for a brief bathroom break. Scheduling a wakeup around three to four hours after going to bed helps avoid a mess in the crate and a pup who howls 4½ hours after you go to bed.

Crate-Training Older Dogs

Older dogs will learn to accept the crate quite readily when it is introduced gradually and positively. The wire crates and shipping crates all come in large sizes and are strong enough to accommodate a grown Rottweiler.

Here is a suggested schedule of training.

- Feed the dog in the crate every day with the crate door left open.
- During the day, when he falls asleep, gently urge him into the crate to sleep with the door left open.
- At night, if possible, put the crate in your bedroom; close the door to the bedroom and leave the crate door unlatched. Make sure the dog has a stuffed bone (see Chapter 5) to chew on.

After a day or two of practice:

- Begin closing the crate door during feeding time. Let the dog out when he's finished eating.
- Take him out to relieve himself immediately after he finishes his food.
- Begin closing him in the crate for the night.
- While someone is home, start putting him in the crate when he is sleepy. Close the door.
- While someone is home, a few times a day, crate the dog. Close the door to the crate and go on about the normal routine. Make sure he has been exercised and give him a stuffed bone. Leave him alone for a half hour.

After a few days of practice, start putting the dog in the crate and leaving the house for a half hour. Be casual and calm about leaving and about coming home.

The more regular the schedule of exercise, crating, and feeding, the more accepting your dog will become.

House-Training

Rottweilers are generally clean dogs and are easily house-trained. While using a crate for the new puppy speeds house-training immensely, there are other factors that go into successful house-training. Apply the following tips, add a little patience, and your Rottweiler will quickly get the idea.

Here are two common house-training myths and the facts about why they are untrue:

MYTH 1: Rub the dog's nose in the mistake.

FACT: If you rub the dog's nose in the mistake, he may assume that relieving himself is wrong and will then decide to sneak off and hide his "mistakes."

MYTH 2: Drag the dog over to the "mistake" and yell at him so he knows he did wrong.

FACT: Doing this can cause the same misguided outcome as in the first myth. Why? Remember that dogs learn through timing and pairing. They cannot relate events that happened minutes or hours ago to the present time; therefore, if the mistake is after the fact, clean it up, and do not punish the puppy. Frankly, these mistakes are your fault for not watching the puppy closely enough.

Technique

In order for a correction to work, you must catch the puppy in the act.

- Get and keep a good schedule with your puppy.
- Take him out first thing in the morning.
- Clap your hands sharply and tell him *"Outside,"* then take him to a designated area of your yard.
- Assign a command to the act of elimination, such as *"Potty,"* or *"Hurry up."* Use one command and stick to it.
- Praise him quietly when he relieves himself in that area. Be aware that many puppies will urinate more than once in a few minutes, so stay out there a while longer.
- Take the puppy out after each meal, each nap, and last thing at night.
- Watch carefully whenever he is playing, as activity often makes a puppy need to eliminate. Watch for sudden sniffing in circles or back and forth sniffing and whining. Get him out right away. Say *"Do you want to go out?"* and guide or carry the puppy outside.
- Always stay with the puppy outside. if necessary, keep the puppy focused by putting him on a leash. Do not allow the puppy to play until he has urinated.
- Do not let the puppy run loose in the house unless someone can watch him closely.
- Put the puppy in a crate or confined area—a baby-gated utility room, for instance—when you can't be home with him.

Troubleshooting

- Clean up soiled spots with nonam-monia-based cleaners. Follow up with a light spray or dab the area with vinegar.
- Limit the pup's water in the evenings and give him ice cubes if he has been playing or seems hot.

Finally, if a pup that seemed well on his way to being house-trained suddenly starts to have accidents, consider the following:

- A bladder or kidney infection. Take the pup to the veterinarian to be checked.
- A change in your schedule or a recent upheaval in your household.
- The age of the dog. Elderly dogs can have problems with incontinence. Also, intact male dogs tend to begin marking territory at about eight or nine months and will invariably start marking the house; females have been known to do the same. Spay-ing and neutering will lessen the urge to mark territory.

Biting

Puppies need to bite, chew, and play; it is very important to their mental health and well-being. Trying to completely eliminate this behavior frustrates this natural desire, which, in turn, increases the problems. There are a number of ways to teach a puppy that biting, chewing, and tugging on certain items are wrong. One way is by teaching a tug-o-war game.

Ideally, the best time to teach this game is as soon as you bring the puppy home. While children can—and should—learn all of the games and handling exercises you play with the new puppy, an adult should always teach the game first and children must be supervised.

Tug-Enough Game

Teaching a tug-enough game does many things for a puppy:

1. It teaches the *enough* command.
2. It teaches that the owner is the leader and controls the game.
3. It teaches the puppy to control his play and bring toys to you, thus avoiding keepaway games.

The best toy to use for this game is a soft toy such as a fleece chewman, or another easy-to-grip item.

- Sit on the floor and engage Fritz in play.
- Entice him to grab the toy.
- Tell him *"Get it."* Do not let go of the toy.
- Pull gently against the puppy.
- Once Fritz is pulling on the toy firmly, say *"Enough"* in a firm, clipped tone. Some puppies may become startled right away and let go. If this is the case, smile and praise.
- Hold the toy away from him a moment or two and keep him from grabbing at it by gently blocking him with your hand at his chest, then present the toy again.
- Repeat the entire procedure a few times in a row.

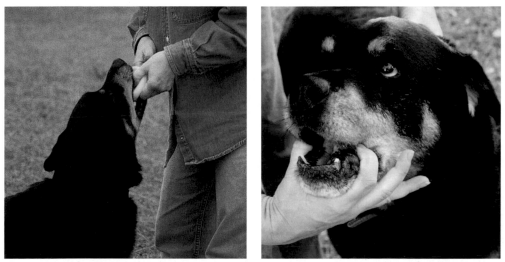

The tug-enough game can be used to motivate during training . . . but your dog must release on command.

If Fritz does not let go when you command *"Enough,"* try the following:

- Immediately take the thumb and forefinger of your free hand and squeeze gently and steadily at the bottom corners of his jaw.
- Press his gums against his teeth. He will then have to open his mouth and the toy can be removed.
- Praise and keep the toy a few seconds, then repeat.

Play this game for approximately five minutes at a time. When finished, simply get up, say *"All done,"* remove the toy, and give Fritz a bone to chew. Allow him to have the toy for a few minutes of play by himself with no more interaction from you. If the toy is one that is not safe to leave him alone with, remain nearby to make sure no pieces are swallowed.

Remember: This is a leadership exercise. Since you are the leader, *you* decide when to start and end the game.

Curbing the Tendency to Bite

This must be done by all members of the family, including the children. Every time Fritz bites someone, make a yelping sound like another puppy would, or make some sort of sound as if you are in pain, such as *"Ow"* or *"Hey."* At the same time, stop all play and interaction. To a puppy, having the play and attention stopped is the worst of all possible scenarios; he then learns that a softer bite allows him to continue playing with his packmates.

If Fritz has become out of control with his biting and no amount of yelping can get him to stop, calmly take time out.

Firmly and quietly place him in his crate for a brief time-out or settle him using one of the handling exercises in Chapter 4.

Chewing

Chewing problems are common with Rottweilers and they are to be expected. The main reason a puppy chews is because he is teething; trying to stop a puppy from chewing will only frustrate him. Instead, supply safe and successful chew toys and teach the puppy that the toys you supply are the only things he can chew.

As mentioned on page 32, one of the best items to use to stop inappropriate chewing is a stuffed bone, which is a real bone that is hollow and has been sterilized and pressure-treated to make it safe and strong. By itself, this kind of bone might not interest Fritz too much, so make the bone appealing by stuffing it with enticing tidbits, such as dried liver bits or regular bits of dog food, to fill the bone up to the top. Use a little peanut butter at the top of the bone to get his attention more quickly. This will rapidly reinforce licking and chewing done by him. A small amount of the food you have stuffed into the bone is fairly easily reached but then Fritz will see and smell even more food inside the bone and continue to chew to try to reach it. Restuff the bones each time you need to leave Fritz in his crate.

Chewing is also a part of investigation for young puppies; they like to wander around and test out the various textures and tastes of household items. Limit your new puppy's access to the rooms in your house by closing doors and closets, and baby-gate him out of or into certain rooms. This way, you can gradually increase his territory as he becomes more trustworthy. Watch him carefully anytime he is freely wandering around your home. Prevention is the best medicine.

Chewing problems are common with Rottweilers.

Grooming and Handling

Your Rottweiler may begin to show his objection to having his feet or other parts of his body handled by growling, pulling away, or even nipping. Be prepared for this and make the commitment to firmly manage any problems right away. Puppies, especially, will learn to accept grooming when you practice every day and insist on good behavior. While your Rottweiler may never actually like being handled, he will at least accept and tolerate this most important part of his training.

Using treats, and starting when the puppy is somewhat tired, spend a few minutes every day doing the following:

- Hold Fritz gently on his side or in a *sit* position and pick up each of his feet, one at a time. After each foot is touched and picked up, praise him and feed him a tiny treat. If he bites at you, say *"Stop,"* and hold the foot a little longer, waiting for a brief moment of compliance from the pup. Then praise and move on to the next foot.
- Lift each ear and look inside briefly while praising, and then feed a treat.
- Gently brush or comb a small portion of the pup's body. When he sits quietly for it, praise and feed a treat.

When these three exercises are done for a few minutes every day you will soon have a Rottweiler who enjoys grooming and handling time.

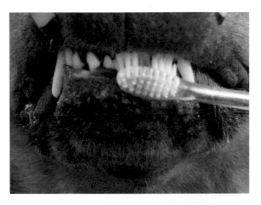

Practice regularly looking at the teeth. Keeping your Rottie's nails trimmed using a grinder or clippers is important and should be done regularly.

As Fritz becomes used to these sessions, gradually add more handling:

- Gently lift the gums at each side of the muzzle and briefly touch a tooth. Praise and treat.
- Hold each foot a little longer at each session and touch each toenail with nail clippers. Praise and treat. If he is calm, try snipping off the tiny point of one or two nails each time you handle them.

- Practice touching Fritz in other areas, such as the genitals and stomach. This will prepare him for veterinary exams. Praise and give him treats for all good behaviors.
- Use the *"Yes"* marker word (see Chapter 4) for exceptional behavior you want repeated during sessions.
- As Fritz becomes comfortable with handling, have all the family members begin the same type of handling.
- When you take him to the veterinarian, have the staff talk to him and feed him treats. Try to take the puppy to the veterinarian just to be weighed and greeted, but always call first and make sure this is okay.
- Take Fritz into the examination rooms and let him explore without any procedures taking place. This will help the puppy learn that it is not necessarily scary to visit the veterinarian.

Jumping Up

One of the most disagreeable behaviors for many owners is having a dog that jumps up on them or on other people; however, this behavior is often started by the owners themselves. When puppies arrive, they are so cute that they are often allowed to develop this habit; it is reinforced when they are picked up or given any sort of attention for jumping up. Remember: Your Rottweiler's growth will be rapid. *Discourage this habit from the very beginning.*

A positive training time for teaching Mollie not to jump is when visitors arrive. Owners frequently disregard this important social time for a puppy, but the more attention you give to this area of training at an early age, the better the dog will behave as she matures. Try to arrange for friends and family to come and greet the puppy often. Flooding her with visits and guests will help her to regard such things as commonplace and will give you plenty of opportunity to practice proper greeting behaviors with her.

Lift each ear and look inside.

If you know when your guests are arriving, be prepared ahead of time. Put on Mollie's collar and leash. When a guest comes to the door, go with her to the door. Have a big smile on your face as you greet the visitor. If the puppy tries to jump up on your guest, gently tighten the leash to keep her off. Have the visitor say *"Off"* and ignore her. If she sits, immediately praise her and have your guest come down to her level and briefly pet her. It is not necessary to have the puppy sit, as long as she is calm and has all four feet on the floor. Encourage the *sit* as you progress and Mollie gets older.

If, at any time, the pup tries to jump, all petting and greeting must stop. The guest should stand quickly, fold his or her arms, and turn slightly away. This is known as *shunning*; however, it is much better to react without any sort of attention, if possible. Mollie should get no reinforcement at all for the wrong behavior and positive reinforcement for the correct behavior. As soon as she is sitting again, the visitor can resume greeting.

Keep Mollie on lead as you visit and give her a stuffed bone to chew on to keep her occupied. If she is terribly excited, try throwing a toy a few times for her to chase. This dispels some of the adrenaline that may have built up and helps to calm her.

If Mollie will not calm down, or if you must interact alone with your guests, put

Jumping up should be discouraged.

her in her crate but within sight of the guests. It is not wise to isolate a puppy or dog from guests. Dogs are pack animals and love to interact. Isolation often causes resentment of strangers and people coming to the door because the dog learns that with visitors, comes loneliness.

7 Obedience Exercises

If the foundation of your Rottweiler's training is leadership, then the mortar that holds it together is obedience. Using basic exercises in the dog's daily training serves two purposes:

1. It solidifies the bond between you and the dog and reminds him who is the leader.
2. It allows you to teach the dog the commands and, therefore, control his actions.

The daily training sessions need not be long or intense; in fact, dogs learn more quickly if the sessions are kept short, fun, and motivational. Keep in mind that more precise obedience and specific exercises will be needed for competition activities (see Useful Addresses and Literature, page 102, for sources to contact regarding competition).

The exercises described in this chapter will give you the control you need for daily activities with your Rottweiler. With practice, it will be a joy to go out in public with him. The best way to enhance the Rottweiler's reputation is to make sure he is represented well to society. That means good behavior, control, and frequent socializing.

Attention, Please

It may sound simple and obvious, but most owners do not have their dog's attention when it counts—during learning and during distractions. If the dog is not paying attention when you are teaching him, he doesn't learn. Also, if he is not paying attention during a distraction, you will not be able to control him. Therefore, one of the first exercises to work on with your Rottweiler is a command that will mean *"Attention!"*

Start slowly and gradually and work for two goals: Attention in the *sit* position with distractions, and attention while moving.

Stationary Attention

Attention while moving is more difficult than attention while sitting. Help your dog to learn more quickly and avoid frustration by teaching the *stationary attention* first.

Step A. Choose a word to use for your attention command; some examples are: *"Look," "Watch me,"* and *"Ready."* Choose one and use it all the time.

Step B. Choose a *release* command. If you have not already started using a word that means *release*, do so now. A *release* command needs to be different from praise. It means that the exercise is over and the dog may break the position he is holding. The same *release* command is used for all the exercises you do with the dog. Some examples are: *"That's all,"* *"Release,"* *"All done,"* *"Free dog."*

Step C. Put Fritz on the leash and collar and place him at your left side in a *sit* position. Fill your right pocket or hand with small bits of tasty treats. Hold your left hand at your waist. Say his name first and then say your *attention* command. When he looks up at your left hand in any way, say *"Yes,"* and feed a small treat from your right hand. If he is still looking at you, praise him and release with the *release* command. If he looks away, say his name again or wiggle the fingers of your left hand. When he looks at the hand, say *"Yes"* and use the *release* command, immediately feed a treat, and move, with the dog, out of position.

Step D. Practice the previous steps every day as many times as possible, making each session short. Do not try to make Fritz hold his attention for longer than a few seconds at a time. When he begins to

> ### TOP DOG TIP
> *Smile and tell Fritz how good he is while he is looking at the left hand. Keep his attention with lots of chatter at first, trying not to repeat your attention command. If he looks away, stop and make a sound such as "Ah, ah."*

immediately look at or touch your left hand when he hears the *attention* command, move on to the next step.

Step E. Begin waiting longer and longer periods before you say *"Yes"* and give Fritz a treat for looking where he is supposed to look. If he looks away, gently tap the top of his head or wiggle your fingers to draw his attention back to your left hand at your waist. Do not immediately give the treat if you have to help him become focused; wait a few seconds longer and, if he remains focused, then say *"Yes"* and give him the treat.

Step F. When Fritz can keep his attention on you for over 30 seconds, begin adding distractions. At first, go back to only a few seconds of attention while adding a small distraction such as someone walking by. Help the dog by encouraging him with your voice. Wiggle the lead a bit or tap his head to get his attention back on your hand. Again, expect only a few seconds of attention when distractions begin and work up to longer periods.

Step G. Continue adding time and distractions to the exercise. When Fritz can

> ### TOP DOG TIP
> *Each time the release command is given, move the dog out of position and praise him. This will teach him more quickly what the command means.*

sit at your left side with attention for up to 45 seconds with distractions, progress to *moving attention (heeling)*.

Moving Attention (Heeling)

■ Begin *moving attention* the same way *stationary attention* begins, a little bit at a time. It is always easiest to start with your dog in the *sit* position at your left side. Use the *attention* command. As soon as Fritz gives you his attention, take a step or two forward while commanding *"Heel."* Keep your movement to only one step or two, immediately give the dog's *release* command, and give him the treat. *"Heel"* will be your command to your dog to remain at your side while you move. The dog will also sit at your side in the same position.

■ The *heel* position means that the dog's head is aligned with your left hip and knee and, if you look down, you can see the dog's eyes. Another good gauge of the *heel* position is

if the dog's front paws are even with your toes as he sits next to you.

■ If Fritz looks away, make the sound *"Ah, ah"* and start over again. Do not reward with vocal praise or a treat. As soon as he moves even a step while still looking up toward the focus area, say *"Yes"* and release him.

■ Increase the number of steps you take a little bit at a time. When you can walk at least 12 steps or more with attention from your dog, add a few light distractions. Just as you did with *stationary attention*, decrease the number of steps when you add a new distraction.

■ *Walking with attention* is different from *loose-lead walking* (see page 51). Use the attention and heel commands—stationary or moving—to keep Fritz near you in distracting situations such as crossing the street, moving through a crowd, or walking past another dog or animal. Use controlled loose-lead walking for regular exercise time and when you have more room to let your dog move out ahead of you on the lead.

Walking on a Loose Lead

As previously mentioned, walking on a loose lead affords a somewhat more casual attitude for you and your Rottweiler. The main goal of controlled, loose-lead walking is that the dog will not pull or lag on the lead and will remain attentive to your commands. He will not cross in front of you or behind you, but will generally stay on your left side as he walks.

Loose-lead walking is best for walks in the neighborhood, the park, or other, wide-open spaces. If distractions arise that require more attention, the dog needs to move quickly to your left side and give you attention when he is told. This is accomplished by giving him the command *"Come"* and then *"Heel"* and *"Sit"* and the *attention* command. He is then in a position to be told what to do next.

To teach loose-lead walking to most dogs, it is best to use a head collar in conjunction with lots of treats, practice, and a longer lead or Flexi-Lead. It is up to the individual owner to decide what loose-lead walking means for his or her dog; however, a dog as powerful as the Rottweiler needs some sort of direction and guidance, or he will take advantage of the extra freedom of a longer lead such as the Flexi. Therefore, when working on loose-lead walking with a Flexi-Lead or long line, the head collar is the tool of choice in most cases.

Heeling with attention to the left hand for a few seconds . . . should be rewarded with a happy release!

Step A. Begin training your Rottweiler in a quiet area of your yard or other familiar place. Place him on the collar and lead. Tell him *"Let's go"* instead of *"Heel."* When used consistently, *"Let's go"* will become a cue to the dog that you are doing a different kind of walking from the closer *heeling with attention* work discussed previously.

Step B. As soon as you begin walking, let Fritz move out ahead of you. If he begins to pull on the collar, say *"Ah, ah."* When you are using a head collar, the work of correcting will be done for you. The dog will pull and his nose will be turned toward you. Immediately let the dog move ahead again. When he is moving ahead but on a loose lead, praise him. Give your *"Yes"* marker (or click) and give him a treat if you wish.

If the dog is not on a head collar or if he is pulling particularly hard, you may try one of the following:

1. Turn and move in the opposite direction from the dog as soon as he pulls.
2. Stop walking and let him pull until he realizes you are not moving. When he turns to see what you are up to, praise and start walking again.
3. Practice calling Fritz to you as you see him reach the end of the leash and just before the pulling starts. This will cause him to begin checking back toward you frequently to see if you are going to call him. Each time this occurs, smile and praise him for checking in. Toss a treat to him or call him to you.

No matter what collar or method you are using, make sure you express your dis-pleasure when the dog pulls. Say *"Ah, ah,"* and begin praising him only when the lead is loose. Practice frequently and be consistent with your commands and reactions. As the dog improves, go on longer walks and start taking him to strange places where there are likely to be distractions. Always be aware that each time you begin training an exercise in a new place, you must start slowly and gradually.

The Stay Exercises

The *stay* exercises are some of the best allies you will have in your control tool-box. A steady *down* or *sit-stay* is invaluable in such situations as greeting people, going in or out of doors, in times of danger, and so on.

Teaching the *stay* to Mollie puts you in charge in situations where she might want to forge ahead or make decisions that will put her or others in danger. A Rottweiler with a strong understanding and mastery of *stay* truly trusts you as a leader. Frequent practice in all positions will help the dog generalize the *stay* command to any position.

Sit-Stay

The first goal in teaching the *sit-stay*, of course, is to teach the *sit* exercise. While this may seem evident and simple, consider that part of the goal is to have the dog sit on the first command.

Step A. Hold a tasty treat in your right hand. With Mollie on lead and at your left

Without the head collar—pull back on the buckle collar and push in at the back of the legs above the hocks.

When the dog's head tips back, she will sit.

side, hold your left hand at her nose and slowly move your hand backward and behind her head. Her nose will follow and her rear end will sink to the ground.

Step B. Say *"Sit"* as Mollie sits, then say *"Yes"* and feed her a treat from your right hand.

Step C. Practice having Mollie sit for her food by using a couple of pieces from the dish before setting it down. Practice having her sit for all attention from strangers or from family members. She will quickly learn that sitting earns attention, praise, and, sometimes, treats.

If Mollie does not sit on the first command, do not repeat the command; instead, help her to understand. Using the head collar, pull gently up on the leash

and lightly touch her rear at the base of the tail. Praise when she sits, but do not give her a treat because you had to help her. The treat and *"Yes"* are withheld unless the dog sits automatically or if she sits on the first command.

If the dog is not wearing a head collar, place your right hand in the flat buckle collar and pull backward while running

---

TOP DOG TIP

You may use a treat in the left hand to lure the behavior, but the treat that the dog is allowed to eat comes from the right hand. This teaches her that her goal is to focus on your left hand.

The *stay* signal.

the leash short, but not tight, give a command and signal to *stay*—your left hand swung down in front of her face with the palm toward her and fingers pointing toward the ground. The command is *"Stay."*

Step B. Stand up next to your dog. Do not step away from her at this time as it is too soon to require distance because she does not yet understand the command. If she tries to get up or lie down, gently but firmly lift her by the flat buckle collar back into the *sit* position without repeating the *sit* command. Repeat *"Stay"* and resume standing next to her.

Step C. When approximately 30 seconds have passed, release Mollie by giving the *release* command you have chosen. Help her to understand how the exercise is done

your hand behind her hocks and folding her into a *sit*. Praise but do not give her a treat.

Stay

Once the dog is sitting quickly and on the first command, begin teaching understanding of the word "Stay." As with any exercise, begin gradually and work up to distance and length of time.

Step A. Place Mollie at your left side and tell her to *"Sit."* Reward her for the *sit* with praise and/or give a treat. With

When first teaching *stay*, remain next to your dog.

Then, gradually increase the distance as your dog learns.

by moving out of position with her with lots of excitement, praise, and a treat.

Step D. Practice steps A through C three times in a row; this gives your dog short, solid successful repetitions of the *stay* exercise . Once you have a solid *sit-stay* for up to one minute with her sitting at your side, begin stepping away from her for brief moments.

Step E. As with all exercises, gradually increase the time you expect the dog to

Gradually increase the distance and duration of time that you leave the dog on a *stay*.

hold the position. Add distractions when the time frame is solid, but decrease the time when you add distractions. Always turn and face her when you leave her on a *stay*.

Down-Stay

The *down-stay* will be taught the same way as the *sit-stay*, except the dog will be in a *down* position. First teach a willing

Keep the treat in front of him and in your hand.

down command before moving on to the *stay*.

Step A. Have Mollie sit at your left side. Hold a treat in your left hand at her nose and slowly move your hand straight down toward the ground. Bring the treat between her front legs and give the command *"Down."* As Mollie follows the treat, she will have to lower her body to the ground. You may help a little by gently pressing on her shoulder blades. Let her think about how to get the treat. Keep the treat on the ground; if you continue to lift it up, she will stand. As soon as Mollie is in a *down* position, give your *"Yes"* or click, and give the treat from your right hand. Release with your *release* command.

Step B. Practice the *down* frequently until you can move your hand down toward the floor and the dog will begin to lie down. This could take days or weeks—be patient.

Patiently wait for your dog to lay down before feeding.

The *down-stay* at a distance.

Step C. Once Mollie is lying down on the first command and without help, teach the *stay* exercise by following the steps for the *sit-stay* exercise.

Stand-Stay

This exercise is a little harder for the dog to grasp, but with frequent practice, it will result in a more manageable dog. The *stand* is not only helpful when grooming, bathing, or having the dog examined by a veterinarian, it also is a required exercise in AKC Obedience competitions (see Chapter 8).

Step A. This first step is the same as in the previous exercises; teach the *stand* first.
Start Mollie in the *sit* position at your left side. Turn slightly toward her, and

place your right hand in front of her nose. You may use a treat to lure, but remember, don't feed the lure. Slowly move your hand straight out and away from Mollie's nose. If she does not seem to want to follow, take a sidestep with your right foot and say *"Stand."* As soon as she stands up, give your *"Yes"* marker and feed the treat. Release immediately with your dog's *release* command.

Step B. Practice daily so that your dog begins to stand up as soon as you move your right hand straight away from her nose.

Step C. Once Mollie is willingly standing up, add the *stay* command. Use the same hand signal and word as in the previous *stay* exercises. Say *"Stay"* and remain

The *stand-stay* takes patience and consistency.

TOP DOG TIP

It is up to you to decide how little movement you will allow during the exercise. Bear in mind that if you think you may someday compete in Obedience, the dog must not move any of her feet during the exercise until you say your release word. This takes lots of patience and practice, but even the pet dog will benefit from being able to stand still for a brief exam.

■ *Sit* and *stay* while being greeted.
■ *Sit* and *stay* at doors.
■ *Sit*, *down*, or *stand-stay* to be brushed.
■ *Sit* and *stay* when putting on the leash and collar.
■ *Down-stay* while you talk with a neighbor.
■ *Down-stay* while you make your bed or fix your breakfast.
■ *Down-stay* while you eat a meal.

As with all exercises, practice daily. When the exercise involves other people, make sure they understand what they are supposed to do in order to make the practice successful. For instance, when practicing a *sit-stay* while being greeted, tell the person doing the greeting to stop petting if the dog gets up.

Once Mollie is comfortable with the exercise you are teaching, take her to an

standing next to her. Wait only a few seconds, then release and praise.

Step D. Gradually increase the time Mollie will stand still, and gradually start stepping in front of and facing her. Practice running your hand down her back, or lifting an ear during the exercise.

Step E. Add more requirements as Mollie progresses. Briefly run a brush down her back or have a friend come over and examine her. Use the command when grooming and bathing her and in other daily situations.

Using the Stay *Exercise*

Using the stay exercise can solidify understanding of the command for the dog. If she is required to stay for short periods throughout the day and for specific purposes, she will learn more quickly. It will also reinforce your leadership position.

The ways to apply the *stay* to daily life are endless. To get you started, try some of the following exercises.

Use the *sit-stay* when greeting people . . .

and when brushing . . .

or when putting on the head collar.

unfamiliar setting and teach it again. Go to parks, practice at the veterinarian's office, go to shopping plazas, but always keep the dog on leash. The object of using the exercises in different places is twofold:

1. You are teaching the dog to *generalize*, which means that the dog learns that the commands you give apply to all areas of her life, not just in the quiet confines of your home.
2. Frequent practice solidifies and hastens learning.

The Rottweiler needs the best public representation from every owner in the country. Think how much better that reputation becomes each time you calmly control and command your dog when she is in the public eye.

Daily practice of *stays* will help the dog generalize.

The recall game is fun for the whole family.

Come-When-Called: *The Recall Game*

Teaching a reliable recall is more than just smart, it is a responsibility and a possible lifesaving exercise. Countless dogs have been saved from running into busy streets because they understand and comply with the *come-when-called* command.

The best way to begin to teach this exercise to the dog is to make it into a game. This game, the recall game, is easy to teach and it works on all ages of dogs.

Of course, the best time to teach it is during puppyhood. If the Rottie is a little older, it may take longer to teach, but the rewards are worth the time and patience.

Not only will this exercise teach Fritz the valuable lesson of coming when called, it is also a wonderful way to provide an outlet for puppy energy. The whole family can play this game at once, making it perfect for teaching children

TOP DOG TIP

At first, it is best to start out in a more relaxed position, such as kneeling or sitting with your legs crossed; however, make sure you help the dog generalize by practicing the game in a standing position once he is playing well.

better ways to interact with the dog. He, in turn, learns to view the children as leaders in the household.

Step A. Have one person hold Fritz by the collar, while the other person goes 10 to 15 feet (3 to 4.6 m) away. Fritz does not have to sit and stay; in fact, the less you require, the faster the game goes and the more fun it becomes for the dog.

Step B. The person who calls first says the dog's name and then *"Come."* As soon as Fritz starts to come, that person praises him.

Step C. As Fritz arrives, that person takes hold of his collar and feeds him the treat. Resist the urge to reach out for him and grab.

Step D. When Fritz has eaten the treat, the other person then calls him and repeats steps B and C. Go back and forth that way for a few minutes.

TOP DOG TIP

Grabbing at or bending over the dog encourages him to stop too far away and possibly play keep-away games.

Frequently Asked Questions About the Recall Game

■ *Where should I play this game?* Always play the game with the dog in the house, or in a fenced area. This will insure that he cannot run too far, should he decide not to come when he is called.

■ *What if my dog won't come to me when I call?* If the dog does not respond to a call, do something to help him out. Go toward him, showing the treat and then run backward and encourage him to come with you back to where you were when you first called. Make sure you move all the way back to that place before you give him the treat.

■ *Why doesn't my dog want to come to me?* Many people often don't realize that they have taught their dog not to come to them by continually applying negative reinforcements when they call the dog. A dog may view many circumstances as negative, and therefore, consider the negativity surrounding being called. Always remember that the dog associates being called with what happens when he arrives, so even if you call him in from play, the association he will make is negative. Another reason dogs may not respond to this command is because the owner has previously chased the dog. Since many dogs find this to be a lot of fun, they quickly learn to move away in order to entice the owner to follow. Turn the tables on this dog by turning away from him first and running the other way.

■ *How long should I play the recall game with my dog?* Begin gradually according to your dog's level of energy and his age. Young puppies can play for about five minutes before they start to lose interest. Build Fritz's interest and stamina as he grows older and stronger; an older dog can usually play for about eight minutes. It is always wise to quit before the dog is exhausted and bored.

■ *Why should I use treats and when can I stop?* Use food rewards 100 percent of the time for every call the dog responds to for the first couple of weeks of training. This establishes a fast, conditioned response to the command. When he is responding on the first call, you can begin to reward more randomly; however, if you completely stop using food rewards, you run the risk of *extinguishing* the behavior. Always use vocal praise and petting to reward, but keep the treats coming too.

■ *Are there other ways to encourage my dog to come running when he hears me call?* Yes. Have someone hold him while you run quickly to a hiding place, then call him excitedly. The person who was holding him lets go and runs with him toward your hiding place, staying slightly behind him. As soon as he finds you, praise him, take hold of the collar, and reward with a treat or his favorite toy.

8 *AKC Obedience*

Overview

Obedience trials and matches are fun and challenging ways to show off your Obedience-trained Rottweiler. One registry that most people are familiar with is the American Kennel Club or AKC (see Useful Addresses and Literature, page 102). There are varying levels of Obedience that include off-lead work, jumping, retrieving, and scent discrimination.

The CD Degree

Obtaining the Companion Dog (CD) degree is an excellent step toward bonding with your Rottweiler through competition and will encourage you to try other activities. The CD is earned by attending AKC-sanctioned trials.

Competitors enter the dog in one of two Novice classes—A or B. The Novice A classes are geared for first-time handlers. Once they have earned the CD title in a Novice A class, all subsequent dogs they train must be shown in Novice B. The exercises in either class are the same. They consist of the following:

- Heeling on Lead and Figure 8 for a maximum of 40 points

- Stand for Examination (off lead) for a maximum of 30 points
- Heel off Lead for 40 points
- Recall exercise for a maximum of 30 points

The above exercises are done individually. There are also the group exercises, done off lead, which consist of the *sit-stay* for one minute and the *down-stay* for three minutes.

A dog will earn his CD when shown under three different judges at three different shows or trials with a minimum total of 170 points out of 200 possible. In addition, at least half of the maximum points for each exercise must be earned.

Exercises

The Heel on Lead and Figure 8

The Figure 8 exercise is executed in the ring using two people (the "posts") spaced 8 feet (2.4 m) apart and facing each other. The handler and dog start by standing approximately 2 feet (61 cm) back from the two posts. The handler, on command from the judge, heels between

Fritz should be standing squarely in stay *for examinations by the judge.*

and around the two posts, forming a Figure 8 pattern. This is done by walking forward and then turning to the left and going around one post; the dog is on the inside. As the handler and dog come around the first post, they then cross between the two posts and go around to the right; the dog is on the outside. At various places during this pattern, the judge will call for a halt two different times. The dog will sit in *heel* position each time. The dog is not allowed to bump, sniff, or show any interest in the posts. The dog must change its pace to match the inside turn—slower—and the outside turn—faster.

If you want to train at home, you can use anything for posts, such as trees, buckets, chairs, and so forth. Eventually, you should use people as the posts to simulate the formal Figure 8 exercise.

Stand for Examination

This exercise is done off lead. You will hand the leash to a ring helper, who holds it for you until you have finished the rest of your exercises. On command from the judge, you *stand* your dog, using a hand signal and/or by lifting or moving him gently into a standing position.

Once Fritz is standing squarely, command him to *"Stay,"* step 6 feet (1.8 m) from him, turn, and face him. The judge will then approach Fritz and briefly touch his head, back, and rump. The dog cannot move any of his feet without a penalty and must not show fear or aggression.

When the exam is finished, the judge will tell you to return to your dog. The dog cannot move until the judge tells you the exercise is finished.

Teaching Fritz the *stand for examination* takes time and patience. The first step is simply to teach the *stand* (see Chapter 7 for more detail).

You can lift him from underneath (gently) while pulling forward on the leash and collar—straight out from him—with your right hand. Carefully place all the feet comfortably and push down on the dog's shoulders to test for movement. Tell him *"Stay"* but do not leave him. Wait a few seconds and then release and praise.

Once the dog can stay for a few seconds without moving his feet, start leaving for very small periods of time; return by moving all the way around him and into *heel* position.

If your dog moves at any time, go back and gently place each foot or the feet again and leave him. Take your time and do not get angry.

As you progress, do the following:

- Gradually work so that you can move to the end of your lead, count five seconds in your head, and then return without the dog moving. He cannot move until you release.
- Once he stays, begin doing an examination as you go back to him. Run your hand from the top of his head to the end of his back and push down just slightly. If the dog moves at all, say *"Ah, ah"* and replace the feet firmly.
- When he does not move as you examine him, have a family member or friend do the examination while you remain at the end of the lead. As the dog gets better and better at staying, have strangers examine him.

Heel off lead.

Heel Off Lead

For the off-lead *heel*, the same pattern is done as the on-lead *heel*, except there is no Figure 8 exercise. Training for this exercise involves the same steps as found in Chapter 7 except without the leash. You will find that the better your dog's *attention* is, the less problem you will have with the *heel* off lead. Practice the off-lead *heel* with your dog for short periods every day, but only once he understands the meaning of *attention* and where the *heel* position is in relation to your body.

Recall

This exercise is the *come-when-called* with a few extras. First, Fritz must come to you and sit directly in front of you, lined up straight. This is often called *front* position by trainers and the command given by many is simply *"Front."* The dog cannot jump on you or touch you. He must remain in front of you until the judge tells you to *finish* the dog, then, on your command or signal, the dog must move to *heel* position and automatically sit. The dog can go to your right and around you into position, or to the left in a small circle into *heel* position.

All recall exercises start with Fritz sitting in *heel* position. Tell him to *"Stay"* and walk approximately 6 to 10 feet (1.8 to 3 m) away, then turn and face him. Teach this exercise on leash first, then move to off-lead practice.

The recall game (Chapter 7) taught your dog how to happily come when called and that is the first step of this

The first step of the AKC *recall* exercise: leave your dog.

When called, the dog comes and sits in front of the handler.

Novice exercise. The next step is to have your dog sit as he arrives at your front, and remain there until you command him to *"Finish."*

To do this, simply command *"Sit"* as Fritz approaches. Point to the middle of your waist to help him line up correctly. Help him by gently taking his collar and lining him up if he does not line up well or sit. Praise him but do not give him a treat; instead, set him up for a *recall* and try again.

Practice short *recalls* a few times a day to help him learn the position you want. In addition, play the recall game during

some practices to keep him upbeat and happy when he runs to you.

The finish of the *recall* can be taught as a separate exercise at first; this will keep Fritz from anticipating the *finish*. Begin by leaving him in a *sit* position but pivoting in front of him so that he is in the *front* position you expect after calling him on a *recall*.

Hold the leash in your right hand at your side and tell Fritz to *"Heel."* Step back on your right foot to help him get moving; this will eventually be phased out since you are not allowed to move during this exercise at a show. Guide him behind you and switch the leash to your left hand behind

A calm, focused dog will always be ready to work.

your back. Return your right foot to its original position as you change the leash so that your feet are even with one another.

Encourage Fritz into *heel* position by using your left hand to guide him forward. Tell him to *"Sit"* before he is able to forge ahead out of *heel* position. Remember to use your marker word *"Yes"* or click the dog for quick and accurate tries. Eventually, fade out the foot movements and other help. The only command you may give in the ring is *"Dog, heel."* Once Fritz is doing this well, take the leash off and gradually work so that he can do the *finish* off lead. You may need to go back to some help such as the foot movement when you begin off-lead *finishes*.

Fine-Tuning Your Exercises

It is strongly advised that you attend competition classes in your area for fine-tuning, rules, practice, and help with problems. While many people manage to train for a title on their own, it is rewarding to train with others for the fun and camaraderie.

Learning about the rules and regulations of AKC Obedience competitions is a must for all handlers. Write to the AKC for a copy of their booklets on Obedience rules and regulations as well as their rules for dog shows (see Useful Addresses and Literature, page 102).

Home Schooling

The training in this book will give you a solid foundation for CD work; you will need to practice at least three times a week in order to make good progress. Training sessions should last at least five or ten minutes. It is not necessary to practice every exercise every time you train; instead, try working on just two or three different exercises each time you go out to train.

Forming Good Training Habits

Day 1: Warm up by playing the tug-enough game (see page 42) with your dog. Get him really interested in the toy. Each time you remove the toy with the *enough* command, have him do something to earn it back; for instance, walk a few steps with Fritz at your left side, or have him sit. Reward him by letting him play a bit after each successfully completed command. End the session on a happy note and put away the toy.

Day 2: Do a shorter warm-up with Fritz, then do a *sit-stay* or *down-stay* exercise. Next, do some *attention*, with Fritz sitting at your left side. You might also practice a recall. Leave Fritz on a *sit-stay* and then call him to you. He sits in front and looks up at you. Release him. Reward him with a treat or toy after each exercise. End the session on a happy note.

Day 3: Start with your warm-up game. Do *attention* work, a bit of heeling, and a recall. Have fun; go for a walk. During the walk, let Fritz go out ahead of you, then call him, and run backward a few steps. Have him sit in front of you and give you attention. Release and continue your walk.

This sample will help you get started teaching your dog to work with you on a regular basis. It is also helpful to prepare for each training session by writing down what you want to work on that day. Gather all your supplies first: treats, toys, leash, and so on. Keep them in a special bag and carry them out to your training area with you. Your dog will love the excitement of seeing the training bag come out; he knows that there are treats and toys in the bag and that fun is on the way.

Proofing

Training for your CD should progress gradually but steadily. Once Fritz knows the basic exercises and is doing them well at home, it is time to start *proofing*. Proofing is an all-important step in the dog's training.

The first step in proofing is simply adding some distractions to your quiet training time; for instance, have family members come out to watch. Have them randomly walk around your training area during *stay* exercises. When you practice attention work in the *sit* position, have someone walk by or stand nearby. Work to improve the length of time your dog will hold his attention on you with more and more distractions.

Some good distractions that will help you prepare for the eventual show ring are rattling keys, food on the ground, people clapping, a loose dog, someone other than

Move practices to public areas such as parks or playgrounds.

you saying *"Down"* while your dog is in a *sit-stay*.

Once Fritz is doing well at home with these distractions, begin taking him to different areas to train. Go to parks, playgrounds, schools, or shopping plazas, always keeping him on lead in these areas. The noise and new smells mimic what it is like at a show environment. Learning to pay attention and work in these areas will help him to view shows as just another place to train.

Do not concern yourself with the actual exercises until you are well along in the basics of training found in this book. Once your dog is doing well with these exercises in different places, move on to the actual individual exercises in the Novice class.

9 *Canine Good Citizen Test*

Owning a Rottweiler means you have an active dog that thrives on fun and work. Training for and taking the test for the Canine Good Citizen (CGC) certificate is a good way to demonstrate the training you've done with your dog. The exercises in this book will help you get started.

Kennel clubs, local specialty clubs, obedience clubs, private training schools, and other organizations, such as community colleges, 4-H, and the Scouts, may administer a CGC Test. Individual dog enthusiasts may also coordinate the event. The AKC provides information kits and test kits for all interested parties. To order your free information kit or to purchase test kits contact the AKC.

Overview and Purpose

The Canine Good Citizen Test is sponsored by the American Kennel Club; it was developed with the pet owner in mind. The test requires that your dog pass ten exercises judged by an evaluator. Each test is designed to assess your control of your dog, your dog's temperament in a given situation, and reactions to everyday occurrences such as the approach of other dogs or people.

This test is a good way to start to become involved in training your dog. By attending classes given by a local kennel club, 4-H club, or other training facility in your area, you will learn how the test is given. You will also acquire the practice you need to pass each test when the time comes.

The CGC is not a competition. Each test is pass/fail and you are allowed to retake the test in six months if your dog does not pass all the tests. Once you and your dog pass the test, you are awarded a certificate that proclaims him a Canine Good Citizen.

The Rottweiler, in particular, will benefit from practicing and training for this test. Classes provide socialization for the dog, the distractions help the handler know where the dog's weak points are, and passing the test is proof positive that the Rottweiler can be a good citizen. Once you have your certificate, you can proudly place the initials CGC after your Rottweiler's name.

The Ten Tests

Test 1: Accepting a Friendly Stranger

This test demonstrates that Fritz will allow a friendly stranger to approach him and speak to his handler in a natural, everyday situation. The evaluator and handler shake hands and exchange pleasantries. Fritz must show no sign of resentment or shyness and must not break position or try to go to the evaluator.

Test 2: Sitting Politely for Petting

This test demonstrates that Fritz will allow a friendly stranger to touch him while he is out with his handler. While Fritz is sitting at his handler's side, the evaluator pets him on his head and body only, then circles him and his handler, completing the test. Fritz must not show shyness or resentment.

Test 3: Appearance and Grooming

This practical test demonstrates that Fritz will welcome being groomed and examined and will permit a stranger, such as a veterinarian, groomer, or friend of the owner, to do so. It also demonstrates the owner's care, concern, and responsibility. The evaluator inspects Fritz, then combs or brushes him and lightly examines his ears and each front foot.

Test 4: Out for a Walk (Walking on a Loose Leash)

This test demonstrates that the handler is in control of the dog. The dog may be on either side of the handler, whichever the handler prefers. There must be a left turn, a right turn, and an about turn, with at least one stop in between and another at the end. The dog need not be perfectly aligned with the handler and need not sit when the handler stops.

Canine Good Citizen Test: Accepting a Friendly Stranger.

71

Test 5: Walking Through a Crowd

This test demonstrates that Fritz can move about politely in pedestrian traffic and is under control in public places. The dog and handler walk around and pass close to several people—at least three. Fritz may show some interest in the strangers, without appearing over-exuberant, shy, or resentful. The handler may talk to him and encourage or praise him throughout the test. The dog should not be straining at the leash.

Test 6: Sit *and* Down on Command/Staying in Place

This test demonstrates that Fritz has had training, will respond to the handler's command to *sit* and *down*, and will remain in place commanded by the handler, in the *sit* or *down* position, whichever the handler prefers. The handler may take a reasonable amount of time and use more than one command to make Fritz *sit* and then *down*. When instructed by the evaluator, the handler tells him to stay and walks forward the length of a 20-foot (6.1 m) line. The dog must remain in place, but may change positions.

Test 7: Coming When Called

This test demonstrates that Fritz will come when called by the handler. The handler will walk 10 feet (3 m) from Fritz, turn to face him, and call him. The handler may use body language and encouragement to get him to come. He may choose to tell him to *"Stay"* or *"Wait,"* or he may simply walk away, giving no instructions to the dog as the evaluator provides mild distractions, such as petting.

Test 8: Reaction to Another Dog

This test demonstrates that Fritz can behave politely around other dogs. Two

A well-trained dog will obey the *sit-stay* command in any situation or environment.

Canine Good Citizen Test: Reaction to Another Dog.

handlers and their dogs approach each other from a distance of about 10 yards (9 m), stop, shake hands and exchange pleasantries, and continue on for about 5 yards (4.6 m). The dogs should show no more than a casual interest in each other.

Test 9: Reacting to Distractions

This test demonstrates that Fritz is confident at all times when faced with common distracting situations, such as the sound of the dropping of a large book or a jogger running in front of him. He may express a natural interest and curiosity and may appear slightly startled, but should not panic, try to run away, show aggressiveness, or bark.

Test 10: Supervised Separation

This test demonstrates that Fritz can be left alone, if necessary, and will maintain his training and good manners. Evaluators are encouraged to say something like, "Would you like me to watch your dog?" and a person will hold Fritz's leash. The dog will be held for three minutes and does not have to stay in position, but should not continually bark, whine, howl, pace unnecessarily, or show anything other than mild agitation or nervousness.

Home Schooling

Preparing for each of the CGC tests can be done at home with the help of friends and family members. It is a good idea to take each test individually and master them one at a time. Practice a different test on each day that you do regular obedience sessions with Fritz. Incorporate the tests into your sessions gradually and build his stamina slowly. Eventually, he must do all ten tests in a row. This will prepare you for the actual test. Remember, testing must be done by a qualified evaluator.

One of the first goals in preparing for the test is to break down the tests to see if Fritz has the fundamentals required. For instance, Test 7 evaluates the *recall* command. For this, Fritz must be able to stay in a *sit* position until called. He must come straight to you when called. Teach this on lead first, as found in Chapter 7. Eventually, the handler must walk 10 feet (3 m) away from the dog. You may leave the long line on him for this test.

Test 6 will show Fritz's ability to obey commands such as *"Sit," "Down,"* and *"Stay."* He will follow each of these commands and then stay in one position or the other while you walk 20 feet (6.1 m) away. He will be on a long line. Break this exercise up into manageable parts before putting the whole exercise together:

- Make sure Fritz will sit on command. During the test, you can give more than one command, but you cannot touch him.
- Make sure he will lie down on command, again, without help in the form of touching.

- Practice leaving Fritz in either a *sit-stay* or a *down-stay* while on a long line. The long line is meant to give the illusion of off-lead work, while supplying you with the means to stop your dog if he should run off.
- Put the three components together once you see that Fritz can do them all. Command him to *"Sit,"* then command him to *"Down."* Now, either command again to *"Sit"* in preparation for your *"Stay,"* or leave him in a *down* position for the *stay*. It will be your choice at the test.

If your dog cannot stay in position when you are 2 feet (61 cm) away, then don't expect him to stay when you are 20 feet (6.1 m) away. Make sure you progress to the required distance slowly. The greeting tests (Tests 1 and 8) both require a few different behaviors from your dog; walking on a loose lead at your side is one. While the dog does not have to be in heel position, he cannot pull on the lead. In addition to walking, he must not jump on the stranger or the other dog in these tests. This means you must have voice control when approaching the other dog or as the friendly stranger approaches you and your dog.

Telling Fritz to *"Sit"* as you approach the other dog and handler and then telling him *"Stay"* will be helpful in managing this test. Of course, *proofing* will be necessary in the form of friends and family approaching your dog regularly while he sits and stays.

As you can see, the *stay* command is one of the most important commands to master. Once Fritz can do these tests at home, make sure you proof him by taking him to parks, playgrounds, and neighbors' yards.

10 *Agility Training*

Overview and Purpose

This sport can give your Rottweiler much needed fun and exercise. He must be at least 12 months old to compete. The purpose of an AKC Agility trial is to give owners the opportunity to demonstrate their dog's willingness to work with his handler under a variety of conditions. The program begins with basic, entry-level Agility and progresses to more complex levels.

The different levels and courses include tunnels, jumps, weave poles, and seesaws.

The dog must navigate the course correctly, off lead and with the handler running along beside him to guide him vocally. Agility is a timed event.

Even though the Rottweiler is a big dog, it is best to wait until he is over two years old before jumping over the required height on a regular basis; growing dogs have enough stress on bones and joints without adding jumping. This doesn't mean you can't start teaching him the many other obstacles that do not include jumping such as weave poles, dog walk, teeter-totter, and others.

It is best to wait until your dog is over two years old before jumping on a regular basis to avoid added stress on bones and joints.

Home Schooling

The Dog Walk

This obstacle can be started with a board cut to regulation length and width (8 to 12 feet [2.4 to 3.7 m] long and 1 foot [30 cm] wide) and laid flat on the ground. In the first step, Fritz simply stands on the board for a few moments without stepping off. Never force him onto the board; instead, have him step on the board with only one or two feet at a time, if necessary. When he does, use your marker word, *"Yes,"* or the clicker and give him a small treat to reinforce that he is right. Proceed slowly until he is stepping on the board with all four feet and calmly starting to walk. Every two or three steps should be marked at first. Eventually, put more and more space between the number of steps taken before marking.

Fritz must also learn to never jump off the side of the board. If he comes off, start him back at the beginning. Do not get angry, but do not reward or treat him if he falls off.

Once he is walking confidently and precisely along the board, raise the height of it by placing a brick or thicker board under the ends of it. Make sure it is extremely sturdy and safe. Continue to raise the board in height as Fritz progresses.

Always have your dog on a leash and his regular flat buckle collar on when working on Agility obstacles that require this sort of control and steadiness. You can use the collar and leash to steady the dog, or to keep him in one spot while you reinforce.

Use of the *stay* command comes in handy for this obstacle. Make sure Fritz gets on and off only at each end of the

Because there are safety issues involved with jumping and running, it is advised that you find a club or training facility to help you train for each obstacle. Have your Rottweiler examined for health problems, such as hip dysplasia and elbow dysplasia, before beginning an Agility course of training. Make sure he is in good condition and not overweight.

Using the training in this book, and a little creativity, you can begin teaching your Rottweiler the Agility course on your own. Remember that puppies should not jump until they are at least 18 months old, and then the jumping should progress gradually.

Young dogs can start on a great many concepts and basics pertaining to Agility without ever having to jump. Older dogs may begin Agility training slowly, and only after they have had a complete checkup by the veterinarian, including X-rays.

Some Places to Start

Even though Agility sometimes looks like a free-for-all, it is actually an event that takes good training and a solid foundation in Obedience. For instance, Fritz must quickly come when called, *down* and *stay*, pause when told, and follow directions with a clear head despite the excitement.

Begin your training by making sure you practice and train until Fritz can respond well to all commands—on and off leash.

Agility is a physically demanding sport. Always proceed with caution and have your veterinarian monitor any injuries.

board you are using. In competition, the ends of many obstacles have a *contact* area that is painted a different color.

This means the dog must touch this area or he will not receive full points. Use a brief *stay* command on this contact area to help your dog learn to slow down at the ends of the boards instead of leaping off.

Tunnels and Other Scary Things

Some of the obstacles in Agility are designed to test your dog's courage as well as his agility. The tunnels are especially

scary to dogs. One is collapsed, so the dog has to crawl through, as if someone threw a sheet over his head. You can begin preparing Fritz for strange and scary obstacles using items found around your home.

Teach Fritz to walk on surfaces of plastic, canvas, and vinyl. Use large pieces of plastic hung over chairs and crawl under them. Drape all different kinds of materials over chairs and crawl over, around, and through them with your dog.

Next, put a piece of plastic over the top of the dog so he can find his way out. Do this only after he displays confidence around the sound of rattling plastic. Always reinforce calm behavior with the marker "*Yes,*" or use a clicker.

A large oil drum or a cardboard barrel open at both ends can start you on your way to other types of barrel navigation. Lay the tunnel on its side and place rocks or other braces on each side so it does not roll when Fritz goes through. Encourage him to sniff and look over the barrel on his own. Praise and mark any behavior that shows confidence.

Once Fritz has examined the barrel, see if he will go into it a step or two. Try tossing a treat inside the barrel. If he goes in to get it, mark the behavior, quickly go to the other opening of the barrel, and encourage him to come the rest of the way through. If he is reluctant, try crawling through the barrel yourself. This will often help the dog see that no danger lurks there.

You can find books and web sites regarding Agility training, rules, and regulations in Useful Addresses and Literature, beginning on page 102.

11 *Carting*

Fundamentals

One of the first jobs a Rottweiler ever had was pulling a cart for his master. Teaching your Rottweiler to pull will provide a much-needed job for him and create lots of fun, as well. Many people make their own carts, but they are also available through catalogs. Your Rottie will enjoy giving the neighborhood kids a ride or helping you with yard work.

Carting, or drafting, as it is called, demands that the dog be in good physical condition. Basic obedience commands are a must. Drafting competitions include obedience exercises in order to demonstrate that the dog is under the handler's control.

Carting involves the purchase or building of carts or wagons, and comfortable harnesses. There are classes, books, and videos to help you decide which ones are best for you. It is important to find and attend classes so that your Rottweiler will learn how to pull without hurting you or himself.

Most places that train dogs to cart insist that the serious training involving weight be delayed until the dog has finished his major growth. Many trainers won't let a dog under 18 months old pull any weight.

Even dogs with hip problems can pull carts, although you will have to learn to limit the work to fit the severity of your dog's problem. As with any dog sport, have your Rottweiler checked by your veterinarian before beginning a program for pulling.

Terms

If you are going to start your dog in the world of carting and drafting, it is best to know the many terms you will encounter. Knowing the differences between types of drafting, carts, and harnesses will help you to make correct choices for your dog's comfort as well as decide the type of carting you wish to try.

- **Draft work** refers to an activity in which a dog pulls something—a cart, a wagon, a sled, or even a log.
- **Carting** refers to an activity in which a dog pulls a wheeled vehicle.
- **Driving** refers to a carting activity in which the person controlling the dog rides in the vehicle being pulled.

Equipment

If you're acquiring your equipment a little at a time, the first purchase to make is a good harness that fits your dog properly. If you are taking part in events, you can

Carting can be lots of fun.

usually borrow a cart or wagon, or switch with someone else's dog, but you need to have your dog's harness fit properly, without chafing, in order to maximize his comfort and enjoyment.

You can start getting a dog used to wearing a harness as soon as he is big enough to fit a harness. Note that many harnesses won't grow as much as your dog will and what fits him as a puppy will be useless long before you can use it for real draft work.

Once you have a harness, you can look into getting a cart or wagon. What you get depends on what you want to do. If you want to haul firewood around, a wagon is probably a better choice than a cart. If you want to carry your kids in parades, then a cart with a seat is probably a better starting point. Most people

seem to end up with a few different vehicles if they become serious about the sport.

Vehicle Types

A *cart* is a two-wheeled vehicle. These may be used to haul freight, while some styles are designed to carry passengers, much like a harness-racing sulky. Since the dog bears the weight of the cargo— freight or passengers—you must be careful to properly balance the load.

Wagons are four-wheeled vehicles. These may carry freight or passengers, and usually have a greater capacity than a cart. The big advantage to a wagon is that the weight is supported entirely by the vehicle; no weight is pressing down

First and foremost, the harness should fit well.

on the dog. It is relatively easy to make a dog-drawn wagon from a child's wagon.

A *travois* is a device without wheels that is dragged by the dog. These are useful when crossing rough terrain. Some are made of wood; others are made of aluminum.

Harness Types

There are several different harness styles. These include parade harnesses, Siwash harnesses, and draft harnesses. Use of one style over another is often a matter of personal preference—sometimes it's your preference; sometimes it's your dog's preference. Mollie will let you know if a certain type of harness makes her happy to work. A dog that doesn't like a particular harness will not work well, and often a change in harness will make her a happy carter again. Note that there are many successful dogs working in all styles of

harness, including "homebrewed" designs. The most important aspect of the harness is that it fits well, whatever the style.

- A *parade harness* consists of a padded strap that goes across the withers and circles the dog's chest, and a second padded strap that wraps around the front of the dog across the forechest. The straps could be leather or nylon webbing, and they are often buckled together. Some find this style of harness may constrict the free motion of the dog's shoulders or legs.
- A *Siwash harness* looks more like a sled dog harness, with a series of straps crossing the dog's back, between two straps that extend past her rear, parallel to the ground. Her head comes out through a padded chest strap that follows down the breastbone and back through her front legs. A belly band provides the connection point for the cart shafts. Dogs have free range of shoulder and leg motion in this type of harness, and most can generate lots of pulling power as a result.
- A *draft harness* resembles the draft rigs normally seen on horses. A large padded collar provides the main pull, allowing the dog freedom of shoulder and leg motion, while also allowing her to lean into the collar with her shoulders and breastbone to increase pulling force as needed. A belly strap provides the shaft connection point, while the traces run back from the collar to the cart. This style of harness is typically made of leather.

Home Schooling

Carting is an activity that Rottweilers enjoy and, when introduced properly, few dogs and trainers have much difficulty learning the steps. The key is patience. With the obedience and behavioral exercises you have taught your dog using this book, you can begin home schooling a puppy or your older dog.

See your veterinarian before starting any physical activity with your dog or puppy. Make sure your dog is in good health and structurally capable of doing what you are asking. Start puppies down the right path for draft work by doing all the steps leading up to hooking them onto the cart, anything short of pulling weight. Any weight should be introduced only to mature, physically fit dogs that are at least 18 months old and preferably 24 months old for the large draft breeds.

Control

Make sure you have control over your dog. The desensitization and handling exercises in this book (see Chapter 4) will prepare most dogs for situations that may arise during carting training. For instance, if you grab Mollie by the collar or scruff to keep her from spooking, will she panic more? Will she try to bite you? Make sure your dog trusts you and respects you and will stop when told.

If your dog is fearful, work on building confidence first, before trying to introduce harnesses and other carting equipment. If you are training an older dog or rescue dog that doesn't know you, and she panics, you and the dog may get hurt. Practice obedience exercises on a daily basis, along with the handling exercises already mentioned. This will help any dog's confidence level.

Happy Dog

Rottweilers generally love and enjoy this work, but must be comfortable in order to enjoy the training. This is your responsibility as a handler. You can start working without owning a harness; in fact, if you have a puppy, don't go out and buy a harness first. Wait until you have an idea how big your dog will get, and also wait until you decide if you will continue the training long term.

If you already have a harness, put it on Mollie and let her wear it around the house while you reinforce acceptance using treats. If she is fearful or worried, play with her while she has it on or feed her and then take it off. Each time you put it on, do only fun things and then take it off before she is tired of playing. She will start to associate the harness with fun. Gradually increase the amount of time she wears the harness.

Generalization

Once Mollie is used to the harness, you want her to learn that she can respond to her obedience commands while wearing the harness. Practice having her sit, lie down, and come to you, as well as stay in all positions. Start with short, easy lessons, and gradually increase the time required to stay.

Take your time, and reward with treats.

Once Mollie is confident wearing the harness, attach the *traces*. These are the long lines you clip onto your harness that eventually connect to the cart or wagon. Let her pull the traces in order to get used to them tickling her legs and sides. You can do this step even without your harness; just attach two long leashes to either side of Mollie's collar and allow her to drag these around as she walks.

Once Mollie is at ease with all this equipment, practice walking beside her. Have a leash on her but try to use it sparingly. Eventually, she will be working with only verbal commands and your leash will not be in the picture. When she is pulling her traces and walking nicely beside you, reinforce her behavior with your marker word *"Yes"* at frequent intervals. Practice changing pace from slow to normal and

make sure Mollie is paying attention to the transitions accordingly.

Using Milk Jugs

Now that Mollie is pulling the traces or long lines well, begin teaching her to be calm despite what is following her. Empty plastic milk jugs can be attached to the long traces. Milk jugs provide a light-weight and safe distraction. Go in a straight line at first and if she doesn't look back or seem to notice she is pulling anything, then add a turn. Make a wide arcing turn but if Mollie notices the jugs without panic, praise and reinforce the behavior. This is the beginning of good control.

If Mollie notices the milk jugs and starts to panic, immediately stop her with her collar and your other hand on her flank. Say *"Settle"* or *"Enough,"* then continue to move almost immediately. Continue a few steps and praise her if she remains calm, then take off all the equipment and play.

During future sessions, follow the same procedure: Stop Mollie from reacting in fear but don't pet her or soothe her for being afraid since that will reinforce the fearful behavior. Instead, move on and praise for the positive, confident three or ten steps she takes after the fear. Do not push her too fast too soon. If you do, you will have a difficult time getting her to trust you and she will be reluctant to work with the cart.

Teaching Pole Acceptance

This step requires someone to assist you. Walk Mollie wearing the harness but with no traces or jugs. Have a friend walk along beside you pulling the cart by the poles. Your friend will say softly to you as you are walking, *"Now,"* and then bump Mollie with the poles gently and lightly.

At precisely the time your friend bumps your dog, you will say *"Good"* and pop a small bit of treat into her mouth and keep moving. If you stop, you will call too much attention to the pole hitting her. Keep moving and, a few steps later, repeat the process. Soon, Mollie will be desensitized to the pole bumps and will equate the bumps with good things, such as praise and treats.

Repeat the entire exercise with you walking on Mollie's right side. There are two poles so make sure she generalizes the bumping to both sides. If she panics at any time, use your *settle* command and a hand at the collar and flank to calm her, and then move on.

The Cart

Once Mollie enjoys and looks forward to the activity surrounding cart training, begin to hook a small practice cart or a regular larger cart to the traces. Go forward with the cart hooked to her only in a straight line at first, then take her out of the cart and do something relatively boring with her such as a *sit-stay* and a *down-stay*. Now, put her back into the cart and do a few more steps and a slow arcing turn. Praise her if she notices the cart; stop her if she starts to worry about the cart. Settle her briefly and then take three successful steps, reinforcing calm behavior with your *"Yes"* or clicker. Remove her from the cart and quit on a positive note.

The younger you start to show your Rottweiler the cart and equipment, the more confidence she will show; however, do not rush your dog or become overconfident about her abilities. At every step of training, make sure you are paying attention and have someone to help you should your dog suddenly become startled or panic. Injuries are highly possible if the dog becomes entangled in traces or tips the cart over.

Important: Get knowledgeable help and good equipment; refer to Useful Addresses and Literature on page 102.

12 Additional Activities for You and Your Rottweiler

Conformation

Conformation shows evaluate and showcase the beauty of the breed. Conformation refers to the physical attributes of the dog being examined and how well they match the written *standard* for every purebred dog. Before you think about showing a dog in these events, it is extremely important that you read and learn the standard for the Rottweiler (you can obtain the information from the AKC; see page 102). While all owners think their dog is the most beautiful, that opinion will be scrutinized closely in the show ring, which frequently results in hard lessons for overeager owners.

The conformation ring at a dog show often looks like ordered chaos. The rules and point system are confusing even for those who have some experience, so it is always best to attend a few shows, join a kennel club in your area, and learn how it all works before you consider entering a conformation show.

Wins accumulated at shows will amass points for the dog and eventually result in

the title of Champion (CH) being placed in front of the dog's registered name. Champions of either sex are considered closely by breeders as possible mates for their own dogs. When looking at pedigrees, prospective buyers will also look for Champion bloodlines, especially when looking for a show prospect. There are three types of shows where dogs can acquire points:

1. *All-breed* shows are open to all breeds that are recognized by the AKC.
2. *Specialty* shows are limited to a specific breed—for our purposes, that would be Rottweilers only.
3. *Group* shows are for all dogs from one of the seven groups, such as Working Group, and so on; for instance a club called "Working Dogs of Any Town" can put on a Group show.

What Is Expected

While Fritz is not expected to perform certain exercises—as in Obedience—training is still important for him to have if you

Conformation evaluates the structure of the dog.

want to enter him in a conformation show. He must stand still and square—this is called *stacking*—so that the judge can get a good overall picture of his balance and proportion. Fritz must allow himself to be handled all over by the judge; this handling includes the genitals. He must also allow his mouth to be opened and his gums to be lifted to examine the correct dentition and mouth pigment.

The handler must learn how to present Fritz to his best advantage in the ring. Gaiting (trotting) must be smooth and fluid with as few breaks in pace as possible. The dog must be patient and under control, since many classes are very large.

If you have purchased a dog that is from show-quality stock, or you feel he is correct in conformation, ask your breeder to help you get started. If your breeder is in another location, get referrals from the breeder to those in your area who might be able to help you.

Showing Your Dog

Some people prefer to show their own dog in the ring. Be aware that campaigning a dog for his title takes a tremendous amount of travel time, grooming time, and preparation, and is expensive as well. Diet and exercise as well as training time all play a huge part in succeeding in the ring. Because of these factors, many owners will hire professionals to handle their dog at shows for them. The dog often stays with this handler for months at a time while he is being conditioned and

This is a Schutzhund Tracking test.

shown. This, too, is expensive and must be entered into carefully.

Before you rush out to begin conformation showing:

- Enlist the help of local breeders who have Rottweilers in the ring and are winning, and ask if they will evaluate your dog. Get a few different opinions if you can.
- Go to conformation shows and observe the Rottweilers. See if you can figure out which dog will win in the classes.
- Ask questions of the breeders or handlers you favor, but do not ask questions when they are just going into or coming out of the ring. Wait until they are taking a break or look them up in the show catalog, which is available at shows at the superintendent's table, and later call them for an appointment.

Tracking

Most Rottweilers love to use their noses. The AKC has Tracking tests all over the country in which handler and dog follow a trail of varying lengths depending on the level of Tracking being tested. Tracking is a time-intensive activity and your dog needs a detailed training program in order to learn to track correctly. As the handler, you will need to practice laying tracks correctly, as well.

In addition to the AKC Tracking tests, there are also Schutzhund tracking tests. These tests are quite different from the AKC tests and learning the rules and regulations of each is highly recommended.

Tracking Games

Aside from competition, you can play fun games with Fritz at any time to encourage

One of the Rottweiler's first jobs was herding animals to market.

him to find you or a member of the family. Starting in the house, have someone hold him while you take a favorite toy and run to another room. Hide behind a piece of furniture or a door, then have the person holding him release him, and encourage him to *"Find."* As soon as he does find you, make a fuss over him, give him the toy, and play with him a few minutes.

Progress to outdoor games in a safe, fenced area or with Fritz on a long line. The person holding him should follow along and be ready to pick up the end of the line if Fritz decides to wander off in some other direction.

To encourage Fritz to use his nose, drop pieces of food as you move away from him. Drop the food in your footsteps, then hide behind a building, a solid fence, or a wall and have your friend tell him *"Find."*

Always let the dog search for each piece of food carefully. Don't rush him, and do not scold him or otherwise correct him during his search. If he is way off

track, just hold the line and wait for him to come back to the track.

If Fritz seems to enjoy these games, advance by going longer distances. You can also have friends or family members do the hiding, or you can hide his favorite toy at the end of a track and then bring him out and see if he will follow your scent to his toy.

Herding

Rottweilers were originally bred to herd animals, chiefly cattle, to market; many Rottweilers today retain the herding instinct. There are a number of different herding tests and trials, as well as organizations, in existence. Many tests will evaluate instinct only. Two organizations that have these tests and trials are the American Herding Breed Association (AHBA) and the AKC (see page 102 for addresses).

The AHBA program offers two types of trial classes, each with three levels. They also offer a test program with two levels. You may enter your dog in the program at any level, and no title is a prerequisite for another; however, once a leg for a title has been earned at a particular level, the dog may not be entered at a lower level on that type of course or that type of stock.

All these trials and tests have set rules and regulations, and training is highly involved and time-intensive. Seek qualified help in your area.

Therapy Work

Many Rottweilers are well suited for service-oriented work. This may mean visiting patients at a hospital or geriatric care facility, or it may involve helping a member of the family who has a disability. This rewarding work is practiced every day by top show Rotties as well as family pets and rescue dogs.

The basics of therapy work include earning a therapy certification through a nationally recognized organization. The dog must pass a test that determines his fitness to interact with disabled or injured people. Tests include acceptance of wheelchairs and crutches in close proximity, as well as reactions to strange movements and sounds that the disabled person may make. Dogs that are granted their therapy license may then go with you to visit sick, disabled, and elderly, lonely people. The dog will have his own identification tag and picture.

Correct screening of the dog and handler is a must for therapy work. Many kennel clubs and obedience clubs are now

This is a Schutzhund jumping test.

offering the training and testing. These clubs work in conjunction with the national organizations that register therapy animals. Check your own local listings for clubs that may help you and your Rottweiler volunteer for these rewarding programs.

Schutzhund Training

Schutzhund training began in Germany in the late 1800s to early 1900s. Contrary to popular opinion, it is not a test of the dog's ability to bite; the main purpose of its development was to test the dog's courage and strength of character. While protection is one part of this test, there are two other sections that are just as important—tracking and obedience.

The dog must complete the three tests of strength and character in one day. Each test evaluates the willingness, stability, and

Schutzhund involves a high level of training in protection and obedience.

temperament of the dog. There are three levels of difficulty in Schutzhund, each of which earns the dog a title in that level. The levels are Schutzhund I, II, and III. The tests of each level involve tracking, retrieving, jumping, heeling patterns, guarding and finding villains, and attacking.

This is a specialized sport and a challenging one. If you are interested in Schutzhund training, be certain that you search for a breeder who has titled Schutzhund-trained dogs in the pedigrees of his puppies as well as the parents. In addition, the breeder can help you find experienced trainers and clubs for learning about this sport. Contact a national club or go online to find out more about trainers in your area.

Rally Obedience

Rally (or "Rally-O" as it is sometimes called) is a new AKC titling event. Competition in Rally is considered to be a stepping stone to the more formal obedience as described previously.

Those that are new to dog obedience are encouraged to participate in Rally as a way of getting their feet wet in the world of obedience competitions.

Rally combines simple obedience commands into a course with signs that tell the handler what to do and where to go on the course. In addition, you are allowed to talk and praise your dog during the exercises.

The dog and handler team begin at the first sign and move continuously through the course following the arrows and instructions on the cards. As with any regular competition, the dog remains at the handler's left side and is expected to be under control at all times.

The titles for each level are Rally Novice (RN), Rally Advanced (RA), and Rally Excellent (RE). Each of these titles is earned by achieving three qualifying scores at three obedience titles. Once earned, the letters can be placed after the dog's name.

There are 10 to 20 cards on each course depending on your level and on the judge, who lays out the course for that competition. Teamwork, willingness, and control are scored. Each card has an instruction that is familiar to the contestant who has worked with a club or trainer to learn what the signs mean.

13 Aggression

Many of the questions asked by new and prospective owners of Rottweilers involve aggression. These questions are important; anyone who owns a Rottweiler needs to have an idea of what to do in situations of aggression. Despite training, despite temperament, dog owners must always be prepared for the unexpected. Here are some of the most common aggression questions:

- What if my Rottweiler growls at me?
- What if my Rottweiler growls at someone else?
- What if my Rottweiler shows aggression toward other dogs?
- What if my Rottweiler is guarding toys or food and won't let me near them?

The Reasons Behind the Aggression

Knowing what is causing aggression is the first step in addressing the behavior. This begins by examining your Rottweiler's training and environmental background. In the case of almost all the situations of aggression mentioned above, explore each of the following possibilities. Remember that more than one factor may contribute to the problem.

Age

The age of the dog in question is one of the first elements to consider. Dogs approximately eight months to two years old go through a number of phases during the maturation process.

Hormonal changes in both sexes often manifest themselves at eight months or earlier, and, in addition, territorial instincts begin to appear. A dog of 8 to 12 months is still immature and cannot distinguish between appropriate guarding behavior and inappropriate aggression. Fear imprint periods also have a distinct effect on behavior at these ages. The fearful dog reacts first and thinks second.

Many dogs will try to challenge their place in the family hierarchy on a regular basis; however, this age period (8 to 12 months) is the most likely time to watch for displays of dominance. Combat the problems mentioned above by attending group training sessions and providing quality, interactive exercise and leadership sessions. These will give the young dog confidence and will emphasize the owner's control.

Gender

While males are typically more likely to display aggression, females have aggres-

You should work hard to socialize your Rottweiler.

sive tendencies as well, but females are less aggressive toward other dogs in most cases. Intact females also may display aggression toward other females.

Both sexes have a marked decrease in all types of aggression if spayed or neutered at about eight months. Spaying will end messy heat seasons, prevent uterine and mammary cancers, and generally calm the female down. Neutering the male will lessen territorial marking, dog-to-dog aggression, and the urge to roam. It will also prevent some cancers. However, neither surgery is a cure-all for behavioral problems.

Genetics

Genetics contribute to the Rottweiler temperament. While temperament problems can be modified with training and environment, there is also an inheritance from the ancestors of each dog to consider. A dog whose parents were aggressive or shy often has the same traits, despite good training. In addition, all dogs have *pedigrees* behind them of dogs with varying

> ### TOP DOG TIP
> *Older dogs may also exhibit aggression. As they age, pain and aching in joints and muscles can make the dog irritable. In addition, their eyesight or hearing will start to fail, causing them to be easily startled. Take the aging Rottie to the veterinarian for checkups more frequently and ask about possible medication that may help relieve pain.*

work backgrounds; for instance, if your Rottweiler comes from a lineage of herding dogs, expect more of that sort of behavior; if the family tree contains a predominance of Schutzhund dogs, expect a higher-energy, high-drive dog. Neither of these is necessarily a bad characteristic, except that this type of dog may not fit your family and lifestyle. Do your research before you get a Rottweiler to help you determine what type of dog you will bring home and be comfortable with.

Degree of Training and Socializing

Even the best trainers and owners sometimes have trouble with their dogs, but it is infrequent and easily fixed because training and socialization are ongoing. Rottweilers that are left to be independent become independent, which means that they will consider themselves the leader in the family relationship and will then begin to take advantage of family members whenever and wherever possible. Unless something is done to change that situation, they will rule the household in no time at all. As with any other behavioral problem, reestablishing your leadership and control is the best way to handle pushy Rotties. Train a few minutes every day, reviewing basic obedience (Chapter 7) and leadership (Chapter 4). Make sure the

> ### TOP DOG TIP
> *Keep in mind that a rescue or older dog that never had any socializing when young will need extra training.*

dog is getting good interactive exercise (see The Recall Game, Chapter 7, and Tug-enough Game, Chapter 6).

Handling the Aggressive Outburst

While knowing the reasons behind the dog's aggression will help the owner understand the aggression, every owner also needs to know what to do during an actual aggressive episode. Each episode is different, of course, and the following will cover the frequently asked questions listed in the beginning of this chapter.

Growling

What if my Rottweiler growls at me?

The first rule to remember in the event Mollie growls at you is to remain calm. If you react by retreating, her behavior is reinforced and she will try the same conduct in any situation in which she wants to intimidate you or get her own way. if you react by screaming at or hitting her, her aggression will likely escalate. If you react by crying and asking "What did I do?" or "Why does the dog hate me?" the learning process will stall and Mollie will continue to take advantage of you.

If the growling occurs in conjunction with territory—food bowl, toy, or bones— it is important that you do not back down. Stand your ground and stand tall. Use your strongest tone and say *"Ah, ah"* or *"Hey"* in a sharp voice. If Mollie reacts by backing off, praise, drop down to her level with a big smile, and call her to you. Ignore the item she growled over. Get her focused on being praised and petted and gradually move her away from the item. Use obedience training to control her while you pick up the item and put it away. For instance, command her to *sit* or *down-stay*. Once the item is put away, bring out a different toy for her to play with. Hold one end of the bone or toy firmly and let Mollie hold one end. Practice the command *"Enough"* that you have used with the tug-enough game (page 42). Repeat this a few times and then allow her to have the bone to go off and chew by herself.

If Mollie does not stop growling when you attempt this method, repeat the sharp sound you made—not louder, just elevate the tone of sharpness. Move your upper body toward her and frown at the same time you make the sound. This body language says *"Leader wants it"* to the dog.

For the dog that is frequently challenging you over toys or bones, it is important that daily work be done toward rectifying the situation. Have Mollie wear the leash and head collar or regular collar around the house so that if she growls, you can easily pick up the end of the leash and direct her away from the item rather than trying to grab her.

Mollie must also have daily work with handling—grabbing her scruff is an important exercise she must learn to tolerate. Go back to using the handling exercises discussed in Chapter 4. Also, make sure she is sitting for her food bowl and sees you preparing the food. Feed a few pieces by hand from the bowl before allowing her to eat.

What if my Rottweiler growls at someone else?

Growling at friends, relatives, and neighbors is usually an indication that the dog has not had enough socializing with people. In addition, the dog's age is important. Dogs that are going through a fear imprint stage will often begin growling or *alert barking* when they encounter people. This is common and does not last long; however, it is no excuse for the behavior. Make sure Mollie is getting more socializing, not less, during these periods—and be sure that it is all positive.

Positive encounters with people will help the dog through the fear stage. Take the dog with you to parks, ball games, and so on. Keep the dog on lead and the head collar on for maximum control. Anyone who wants to greet Mollie can toss a treat to her. Praise her for all nonaggressive behavior. Smile at the person and talk for a few minutes, even if Mollie indicates she does not want to be petted. Keep the dog in a *sit-stay* position at your side. If she allows the person to approach without growling, reward her with praise and a treat. Have the person also feed a treat and pet the dog on the chest. Remind the dog to *"Stay."*

At your home, enlist the help of neighbors, children, and friends to come over to the house for dog-greeting time. Have Mollie wear the head collar and a leash so that, as soon as someone arrives, you will be in control. Use the same approach just described. Keep Mollie beside you while everyone visits and relaxes. Once relaxed, allow her to visit with people as long as she is nonaggressive. Have the guest throw a toy for her to chase. This will

---

TOP DOG TIP

A good rule of thumb is this: Anything that is hard for your Rottweiler to deal with needs to be done more, not less. Grooming and handling the feet, ears, teeth, and mouth, as well as nail trimming, accomplish more if practiced every day. Even if you do only one nail a day, it will help to teach Mollie to tolerate what she does not like but needs to have done.

---

dissipate the energy that builds up during stressful situations and help her to relax more. Reward all good behavior with treats and praise.

Aggression Toward Other Dogs

What if my Rottweiler shows aggression toward other dogs?

Growling or barking at other dogs is a typical reaction for many Rottweilers. Whether male or female, it is often a territorial attitude. Socializing the dog well around other dogs will help, but some dogs never quite get over this annoying and frustrating behavior.

It is important that Mollie realize this is unnecessary and unacceptable behavior to the pack leader (that's you); therefore, learn to recognize your dog's particular body language in these situations.

Some of the more common body postures to watch for are:

- Mollie stands high on her toes and stiffens her body, raising the fur

along her back and neck, with her ears flashing forward.
- She may growl very low in her chest.
- Don't wait for any other signs than these; once your dog starts lunging and barking, it will be much more difficult for you to regain control.

Be calm when Mollie begins posturing toward another dog. Calmly take her scruff and say *"Stop"* or *"Quiet."* It helps to use the head collar on walks so that the control over her is steady. Give her a command to help get her focused away from the other animal; for instance, give your *attention* command and then turn away from the other dog. Keep Mollie moving past or away from the distraction with lots of chatter. Keep your voice firm and calm. Praise her when she is calm and quiet.

Teaching a Quiet Command

Teach Mollie a *quiet* command. When you say *"Quiet,"* say it in a clipped, sharp tone. If she is not immediately quiet, circle her muzzle with your fingers and repeat the command (see Chapter 4, Handling Exercises). Praise Mollie when she is *quiet*.

Another helpful solution in teaching a *quiet* command is to use a squeeze bottle of lemon juice purchased at your grocery store. If you command your dog to be quiet and she does not comply, calmly open her mouth and squirt some lemon juice at the very back of her throat. Do not yell or chastise her. This will teach her

The *quiet* command can be used to silence a barking dog.

that there is a very unpleasant consequence if she does not follow your *quiet* command; it also has the effect of quieting the dog immediately. This is where you come in with praise and more praise for being quiet. After Mollie has gotten over the shock of it all, and if she is still quiet, give her a treat.

Finally, When your Rottweiler shows aggression, make sure you are not inadvertently encouraging her to continue.

Many owners do this by stroking the dog and saying soothing things like *"It's okay. Good dog."* Well, it is *not* okay, and she is certainly *not* a good dog when she growls and barks. Do not pet her when she is aggressive or scared; it will only serve to reinforce the behavior.

As with all of these situations, follow through afterward with more exposure and training around distractions, other dogs, and people.

14 Rescued Rottweilers

Unscrupulous Breeders

No discussion of today's Rottweiler is complete without mentioning rescue efforts and the ongoing battle to save unwanted and mistreated dogs. In 1997, the Rottweiler was ranked number 2 on the AKC's list of most popular breeds. Conversely, in the year 2007 the Rottweiler was 15th on the list. Breeders and owners alike should be thrilled that this ranking has changed, as with popularity comes overbreeding and unscrupulous breeding.

Less popularity does not necessarily mean that the breed has been improved. Unfortunately, some people only want to ride the wave of popularity and make money from breeding Rottweilers, with no thought to temperament or the genetic diseases so prevalent in the breed. These same breeders will sell dogs to anyone who has the money. Since they do not care where the dogs go, buyers may perpetuate bad temperaments and physical problems by breeding the dog they have purchased. This circle of breeding goes unchecked and results in the large numbers of dogs seen at animal control and humane societies.

Bad temperaments also contribute to the large numbers of dogs that may bite or attack people. This does nothing to improve the reputation of the Rottweiler. Until the numbers of Rottweilers being bred drops and the breedings themselves are based on knowledge of the breed, the numbers of dogs getting into trouble will rise.

A Helping Hand

Fortunately, there are individuals and organizations that devote their time, energy, and money to rescuing and rehabilitating as many Rottweilers as possible. With donated money and often with their own savings, they provide love and healing for these dogs. Some dogs must be euthanized right away due to illness or injury; others have been abused so badly they will never be safe among people again. Those difficult decisions are made every day; it is heartbreaking work.

The lucky ones are nursed and cared for by kind, caring individuals. Through a network of clubs and the Internet, potential homes are evaluated by volunteers and transportation is provided, if necessary, from state to state.

Each Rottweiler is evaluated by the rescue organization for stable temperament. The dog is tested to find out if it likes children, other animals, and so on. Then each dog is matched to a potential adopter based on the dog's character and the adopter's needs and wants. When the dog is deemed healthy, it travels to its new and permanent home. All animals are spayed or neutered before they can be adopted. There is a nominal fee charged to cover the costs of veterinarian bills and transport.

There are many ways to help these hard-working organizations and help Rottweilers. While money is deeply appreciated, so are any of the following:

Volunteer to help Rottweiler rescue.

- Time! Volunteer to help a rescue shelter to clean, bathe, walk, groom, or play with the animals. Help clean kennels and runs. Typing information packets, stuffing envelopes, and running errands are helpful chores.
- Food and other necessities are always needed. Donate a bag of dog food a month, old towels, sheets, or blankets, toys, leashes, collars, and other supplies.
- Crates. Wire and airline shipping crates—medium- to large-sized— are usually needed.
- Foster home. This is a little more time-intensive but gratifying. The valuable space and time you can provide in your home for a rescued Rottweiler is priceless. When the dog is adopted, the hard part is letting it go, but, unfortunately, there always seems to be a waiting list of more animals up for adoption. Make sure the rescue organization has evaluated the foster dog for temperament and health problems.
- Adoption. This is the ultimate gift. If you have the time and space, and are approved by the rescue organization, one of these special Rottweilers is a welcome addition to any home. All organizations screen potential homes and match dogs and new owners carefully.

Almost every rescue organization in this country has a full house. Homes are needed every day, every minute. The best way to find out if you can help in any way is to call or write one of the rescue

Foster care is important to rescue organizations.

organizations listed in Useful Addresses and Literature, page 102.

YOUR RESCUE BOX CONTENTS

- *canned dog food*
- *small box biscuits*
- *safe toys*
- *towels*
- *old bedding*
- *coupons for dog food*
- *collars your puppy outgrows*
- *extra leashes*
- *small bag of dog food*
- *stamps*
- *envelopes*

Training Advice to Use for Rescued Rottweilers

Many people are discovering the joys of Rottweiler ownership by adopting rescue cases; however, many owners of such dogs avoid obedience training for fear of *stressing* the dog. Or they may feel that the dog won't like them if he or she is made to do obedience. Nothing could be further from the truth and nothing could be more detrimental to the well-being of the dog.

In order to bond with a rescued dog, more than plain old love is necessary; establishing a leadership relationship is also important. While this is true with any dog/owner relationship, it is particularly important with rescues.

Because rescued dogs have usually been ignored, and possibly abused, by previous owners, it is crucial that they understand you will be fair to them. They must learn to respect your decisions within the family as final. While Rottweilers are independent, rescues are often more independent because of the necessity of having had to fend for themselves in most situations.

Many dogs will continue to assume that they must think and act for themselves unless they are given the opportunity to realize that you will now take over. Assume an attitude of benevolence toward the dog.

Conversely, the rescued Rottweiler may be extremely clingy and shy. It is not necessary or prudent to dwell on the dog's past abuse by spoiling him. Either way, giving these rescued dogs confidence through positive training will help.

All rescued dogs will benefit from the training and handling exercises in this book, but a little more time and patience may be necessary. Bear in mind that there are always exceptions to the rule. Use caution and respect when attempting new exercises.

It is highly recommended that you enroll the dog in a reputable dog obedience class. Look for a well-run class that teaches the basics and practical applications of dog obedience. One of the exercises that you can begin practicing with the dog every day involves getting acquainted with or bonding with the dog.

The Bonding Exercise

Sit on the floor with your dog. If he is too exuberant, sit in a chair. Have some tasty treats easily accessible. Talk softly to him, giving no specific command. Encourage him to look at you by praising him and smiling. Feed a treat and praise him when he looks at you. Lovingly speak to him for a few minutes, two or three times a day, feeding treats only when he is looking at your face.

If the dog is pushy, hold him back from jumping on you by keeping a hand on his collar. Ignore him and do not praise or treat him if he is jumping up or is not looking at you. Continue this for at least

two weeks. This will lay the groundwork for the *attention* command (see page 48), which is important to all obedience work. Encourage all members of the family to do this with the dog. And remember, always supervise children when doing this or any other exercise.

Legislative Issues Concerning Rottweilers

Legislation concerning the banning or restriction of Rottweilers is being proposed or has been enacted in many cities in almost every state. Owners of Rottweilers everywhere need to be aware of the laws in their state and specific city. While this may not seem necessary, you will be surprised by the number of cities that have already banned this breed. They are listed at the end of this section.

To be useful, legislation must be effective, enforceable, economical, and reasonable. In many cases, legislation is motivated by fear and lack of relevant knowledge; worst of all, banning will not solve the problems. What is truly needed instead of bans and restrictions is education for responsible ownership.

The fact is that there is no relationship between the breed of the dog and the number of incidents. Consider this: If your town has 100 German Shepherds and one Poodle, you'll soon learn that the German Shepherds are responsible for 100 times as many incidents as the Poodle. Does this mean that all German Shepherds are vicious? Of course not.

Rottweiler owners need to be aware of their local laws concerning this breed.

Taken as a whole, the Rottweiler breed has continually proven its stability and good canine citizenry by becoming Search and Rescue dogs, therapy dogs working inside hospitals, herding or carting dogs, and family companions.

A five-year study published in the *Cincinnati Law Review* in 1982, which specifically considered Rottweilers, concluded in part that ". . . statistics do not support the assertion that any one breed was dangerous ... when legislation is focused on the type of dog it fails, because it is . . . unenforceable,

confusing, and costly . . . focusing legislation on dogs that are 'vicious' distracts attention from the real problem, which is irresponsible owners."

What You Can Do

If your town, city, or state is considering breed-specific legislation against Rottweilers, speak up and fight back.

■ Write to newspaper editors, your senators, and city council.

- Attend all meetings on the proposed bill and get support from other animal owners.
- Vote against current legislation that is contrary to fact and distracts from the real issue—responsible ownership.
- Work to establish reasonable guidelines for responsible pet ownership, and encourage legislation that supports owner responsibility without reference to specific breeds.
- Keep up-to-date by frequently visiting the web site given at the end of this list. If you have information regarding your town's law, inform the site owner.
- Each state and town has varying reasons for the ban or restriction on this breed. In many cases, it stems from a bite incident; however, in some, it may simply be a case of someone who complained that they were frightened by a dog that may or may not have been a Rottweiler. Penalties for owning a Rottweiler in these areas also vary. It is important that you contact local and state government offices and ask where you can obtain a copy of the dog laws in your area. If there are already bans in place, find out the specifics of the penalties.
- If there is proposed legislation, attend some council meetings to find out what the changes will entail. Try to become involved in keeping track of your county and city laws regarding legislation.

Below is a list of some of the areas of the country that have banned or restricted Rottweilers. This list is provided by Jan Cooper and can be accessed on her web site. It is constantly being updated and she also posts news regarding pending legislation (*www.rott-n-chatter.com/rottweilers/lawslbreedspecific.html* or *www.amrottclub.org*).

IOWA
Conrad

KANSAS
City of Inman

MISSOURI
Carl Junction

NORTH DAKOTA
Velva

SOUTH CAROLINA
Traveler's Rest

UTAH
Smithfield

WASHINGTON
Neah Bay

The following cities have restricted Rottweiler ownership:

ARKANSAS
North Little Rock

NEW YORK
Binghamton

Useful Addresses and Literature

Organizations

American Kennel Club (AKC)
AKC Operations Center
8051 Arco Corporate Drive, Suite 100
Raleigh, NC 27617-3390
(919) 233-9767
www.akc.org

American Rottweiler Club
Gwen Chaney, President
18182 E. Euclid Place
Aurora, CO 80016-1100
(317) 280-1235
www.amrottclub.org

Schutzhund Organizations

DVG America
Secretary: Sandi Purdy
2101 S. Westmoreland Road
Red Oak, TX 75154
(972) 617-2988
www.dvgamerica.com

Agility Associations

The North American Dog Agility Council
(NADAC)
P.O. Box 1206
Colbert, OK 74733
www.nadac.com

United States Dog Agility Association, Inc.
(USDAA)
P.O. Box 850955
Richardson, TX 75085-0955
(972) 487-2200
www.usdaa.com

Therapy Training and Testing

Therapy Dogs International, Inc.
88 Bartley Road
Flanders, NJ 07836
(973) 252-9800
www.tdi-dog.org

Web Sites

Agility

www.cleanrun.com

www.nadac.com

www.dogpatch.org/agility

Carting

www.dogworks.com

www.doginfomat.com/dog09a.htm

Herding

www.ahba-herding.org

www.herdingontheweb.com

Rally

www.canismajor.com/dog/rallyo.html

www.akc.org/events/rally/index.cfm

www.rallyobedience.com

Rescue and Breed Legislation

www.geocities.com/Petsburgh/7568/rescuelinks.html

www.stopbsl.com

www.rottrescue.org

Therapy Training

www.deltasociety.org

www.therapydogs.com

www.tdi-dog.org

Tracking

www.canismajor.com/dog/nose.html

www.ussartf.org/dogs_search_rescue.htm

www.dogplay.com/Activities/tracking.html

Books and DVDs

Simmons-Moake, Jane. *Excelling at Dog Agility, Book 1: Obstacle Training.* Houston, Texas: Flash Paws Productions, 2005.

Simmons-Moake, Jane. *Agility Training: The Fun Sport for All Dogs.* New York: Howell Book House, 1992.

Bauman, Diane. *Agility Start to Finish.* Loveland, CO: Alpine Publications, Inc., 2008.

Breed Specific

Hustace-Walker, Joan. *Rottweiler Handbook.* New York: Barron's Educational Series, Inc., 2001.

Klem, Joan and Susan Rademacher. *The Rottweiler Handbook.* New York: Howell Books, 2001.

Conformation

Alston, George. *Winning Edge: Show Ring Secrets.* New York: Howell Book House, 1992.

Coile, D. Caroline. *Show Me! A Dog-showing Primer.* New York: Barron's Educational Series, Inc., 1997.

Brucker, Jeffrey. *Preparation and Presentation of The Show Dog (DVD).* Self-published: 2004.

Herding

Holland, Vergil. *Herding Dogs, Progressive Training.* New York: Howel Book House, 1994.

Obedience

Handler, Barbara. *Successful Obedience Handling, 2nd Edition.* Loveland, CO: Alpine Publishing, 2003.

Bauman, Diane. *Beyond Basic Dog Training, 3rd Edition.* New York: Howell Book House, 2003.

Pryor, Karen. *Don't Shoot the Dog.* New York: Bantam Books, 1999.

Tracking

Johnson, Glen R. *Tracking Dog: Theory and Methods, 5th Edition.* New York: Arner Publications, 2003.

Ganz, Sandy and Susan Boyd. *Tracking From the Ground Up.* St. Louis, MO: Show-Me Publications, 1992.

Schutzhund

Dildei, Gottfried, and Sheila Booth. *Schutzhund Obedience: Training In Drive.* London, UK: Podium Publications, 1992.

Rally

Kramer, Charles (Bud). *Rally-O: The Style of Rally Obedience, 3rd Edition.* Manhattan, KS: Fancee Publications: 2005.

Dearth, Janice. *The Rally Course Book–A Guide to AKC Rally Courses.* Loveland, CO: Alpine Publishing, 2004.

Glossary

Agility: AKC-recognized sport for all breeds and mixes of breeds; involves courses that are run by the dog and handler. Obstacles include weave polls, jumps, seesaws, and tunnels.

Alert barking: Type of barking that begins around the age of seven to nine months; warns of an approaching person or other thing unknown within the dog's sight range; usually a short, sharp bark accompanied by raised hair on the back.

American Kennel Club (AKC): World's largest purebred registry. Seeks to educate owners regarding responsible ownership. Noted for education, research, and advancement of the purebred dog. Regulates over 15,000 dog events every year.

American Rottweiler Club (ARC): Organization dedicated to educating the public about responsible breeding and care of the Rottweiler.

Attention: Specific command that requires the dog to look up toward the owner during training exercises; essential for true learning to take place. Attention is taught first while stationary, and then while moving.

Bonding: Forming of a relationship between canine and human; achieved through training, play, and specific exercises.

Carting: Utilitarian and recreational pastime of many dogs and owners that involves teaching the dog to pull a cart. The dog is directed via handler commands from the side; some carts are built to be driven by the handler, who uses reins to control the dog.

Clicker: Small noisemaker that has a distinct, consistent, clicking sound; used as the conditioned reinforcer to mark behaviors.

Conditioned reinforcement: Also known as CR; a specific word or sound that is immediately followed by food or other motivator. Conditioned reinforcements are used to mark correct behaviors.

Contact area: In Agility, the area of certain obstacles that is a different color from the rest of the obstacle. This is the area the dog must touch in order to earn the points for completing the obstacle.

Cradling: Handling exercise that teaches puppies to lie quietly and respect restraint. The puppy is held on its back in the arms, as one holds a baby.

Desensitization: Method used to help dogs overcome the fear of being touched. Food rewards are offered for calm, quiet acceptance of touching or holding certain parts of the body such as the feet, teeth, or ears.

Dominance: Behavior characteristics displayed by some dogs; these include boldness, stubbornness, unwillingness to follow, and the need to be in charge; not necessarily a negative trait.

Extinguish: To completely stop or lessen considerably those behaviors that are not reinforced or rewarded.

Fear imprint period: Age period when a dog may suddenly fear objects, people, and noises. Most dogs experience one or more of these periods before the age of two years.

Flexi-Lead: Long line encased in plastic used for walking dogs; allows more exercise for the dog and is helpful in teaching commands at further distances than the 6-foot (1.8-m) lead.

Flight instinct period: Age period when a dog is likely to begin running away from its owner, testing leadership, and is entering adolescence.

Flooding: Repeatedly exposing a dog to stimuli in a positive manner; helps to accustom the dog quickly to frequently occurring stimulations such as greeting people, loud or repetitive sounds, other dogs, and other animals.

Generalization: Act of teaching a dog that commands are to be followed the same way in different areas; for example, the *down* or *sit-stay* commands must be obeyed at home, at the park, at the veterinarian's office, and so on. Many dogs that do a perfect *sit-stay* at home cannot do the same exercise anywhere else until they receive this training.

Head collar: Gentle collar system used to control the dog instead of choke or other metal training collars; controls the dog through firm control of the head instead of the neck; works using communication at the pressure points dogs instinctively use on each other.

Heel: Specific command and position for a dog in which the dog will sit or walk at the handler's left side with its head and neck in alignment with the handler's left hip. In this position, the dog will give full attention to the handler and remain close until released; different from loose-lead walking.

Leadership training: Training that emphasizes teaching a dog to accept and tolerate restraint aimed at control; includes frequent exercises involving handling the feet, ears, and teeth, inverting the dog, taking hold of the scruff, and laying the dog on its side.

Loose-lead walking: More relaxed walking with the dog on lead, allowing it to go ahead of the handler on exercise-oriented walks. The dog will neither pull nor lag on the lead, will remain attentive to commands, and will not cross in front of or behind the handler, but will generally stay on the left side as it walks.

Lure: Piece of food used to guide a dog into a desired position such as the *sit*. When used correctly, the lure is not fed to the dog; instead, the handler gives the dog a smaller piece of food with the opposite hand, which teaches the dog that the true reward does not have to be seen in order to be earned.

Marker: Word or sound used to indicate to a dog that its behavior is correct at

the moment it displays the behavior the handler likes. The word or sound must be the same each time and in this text the marker word is *"Yes."* The marker sound is made with a clicker.

Motivation: Food or toy that is used to reinforce and reward good behaviors.

Operant conditioning: Science of training animals using reinforcement that occurs during a response. This has a direct bearing on future responses; for instance, if a treat is given at the exact moment a dog comes to the handler when called, the dog is more likely to come when called the next time. Conversely, if a negative is applied—bath, punishment, and so on—the dog is less likely to repeat the behavior the next time it is called.

Pack drive: One of the drives of the dog; instinctual need to be with members of a unified pack; used in training through leadership exercises with the dog.

Prey drive: Instinctive need in dogs to chase, catch, and hold moving items. This can refer to toys, animals, and so on; often a strong drive in Rottweilers;

used in training to reward the dog for certain behaviors by throwing a ball or other toy.

Reinforcement: Positive or negative attention given during a behavior that is aimed at either increasing or decreasing the behavior's occurrence. In order to be a true reinforcer, it must be given at the time of the behavior.

Schutzhund: German sport first used to evaluate a dog's steadiness, character, and temperament for working; includes obedience, tracking, and protection phases.

Scruff: Area of loose skin at the back of the dog's neck. In training, a firm hold on this loose skin can help control and calm the dog.

Settle: Handling command given when the handler is firmly and quietly holding the dog on its side in order to teach it to respect restraint and the owner's leadership.

Shaping: Changing behaviors in small increments; achieved through reinforcement schedules—usually with food—that gradually demand more from the dog before the reinforcement arrives.

Shunning: Teaching a dog to stop behavior such as jumping; involves the handler consistently turning away, giving no eye contact, and folding arms during the dog's jumping. The handler gives the dog praise as soon as it stops the behavior.

Socialization: Important training for the health and well-being of a puppy; includes positive experiences at the earliest age possible with exposure to strangers, noises, certain objects, and other animals.

Standard: Written qualifications for each AKC-recognized breed developed by breed clubs and used to judge dogs at conformation shows. Official standards require dogs to match as closely as possible the standard's requirements for temperament, character, color, movement, and structure.

Stop: In reference to conformation, the area just below the eyes of the dog where the muzzle starts; also used in handling exercises to teach the dog to accept control.

Stuffed bones: Hollow, real bones found in pet catalogs and stores. When filled with liver, cheese, or other food items, they offer the dog much to chew and keep busy in the crate or while alone in the house.

Submission: Position of a dog that involves lying on its back with its feet in the air, flattening its ears, and avoiding eye contact. Submission exercises help the puppy understand and accept leadership without fear; a puppy or dog shows submission during compliance.

Traces: Lines that attach a cart to a harness; used in draft work.

Tracking: Activity that uses the dog's superior sense of smell; involves following tracks laid by a stranger or the handler. The dog and handler team must then follow the track correctly, with the dog often required to find an item or items left along the trail to be picked up by the handler.

Index

A
Adoption, 97
Age, 90
Aggression, 90–95
Agility training, 75–77, 102
Alert barking, 93
All-breed shows, 84
American Kennel Club, 7,
    62–69, 102
American Rottweiler Club, 7,
    102
Attention
  moving, 50
  stationary, 48–50
Attention training, 24–25

B
Backyard breeders, 6
Bans, 99, 101
Barking, 93–94
Bedding, 39
Behaviors, 4
Biting, 20, 42–44
Bonding, 98–99
Bones, 32, 44
Breeders, 5–7, 96

C
Canine Eye Registration
    Foundation, 6
Canine Good Citizen,
    70–74
Carting, 78–83, 103
Character, 3
Chewing, 44
Children, 18–20
Clicker, 23–24, 76
Collars, 29–30

Collar training, 37
Come-when-called, 34,
    60–61, 64–66
Commands
  come-when-called, 34,
      60–61, 64–66
  down-stay, 56–57, 72
  quiet, 94–95
  settle, 26–27
  sit-stay, 52–54, 72
  stand-stay, 57–58
  stay, 52, 54–56, 58–59
Companion Dog, 62–67
Conditioned reinforcement,
    21
Conformation, 84–85
Corrections, 41
Cradling, 25
Crate-training
  of older dogs, 40–41
  of puppies, 38–40
Crowd, 72

D
Desensitization, 24
Distractions, 73
Dominance
  leadership vs., 28
  social, 10, 12, 14
Down-stay, 56–57, 72
Draft harness, 80

E
Elevation dominance, 10,
    12, 14
Equipment
  collars, 29–30
  leash, 29

Extinguish, 61
Eyes, 6

F
Fear imprint period, 9
Females, 90–91
Flexi-Lead, 29–30
Flight instinct period, 9
Following, 10–12, 14
Food, 24, 33–34

G
Gender, 90–91
Genetics, 91–92
Grooming, 45–46, 71
Group shows, 84
Growling, 4, 92–94
Grumble, 4

H
Handling, 19, 25, 46
Harness, 80
Head collars, 30, 53
Heel, 50, 62–64
Herding, 87–88, 103
House-training, 41–42

J
Jumping up, 46–47

L
Leadership, 27–28
Leash, 29
Leash conditioning, 37–38
Leash training, 37
Legislation, 99
Loose-lead walking, 51–52,
    71

M
Males, 90–91
Marker, 21–23
Moving attention, 50
Muzzle hold, 26

N
Name, 36
Negative reinforcement, 34
Neonate, 8–9
Neutering, 9, 91

O
Obedience
  AKC, 62–69
  exercises for, 48–61
Older dogs
  crate-training of, 40–41
  grooming of, 46
Operant conditioning, 21–28
Organizations, 102
Orthopedic Foundation for
    Animals, 6, 8
Other dogs, 94

P
Pack drive, 28
Parade harness, 80
Pedigree, 91
Personality traits, 3–4
Petting, 71
Playing, 27
Popularity, 96
Positive reinforcement, 21
Prey drive, 18
Proofing, 68–69
Puppy
  biting by, 42–44
  from breeders, 5–7
  crate-training of, 38–40

developmental stages of,
  8–9
finding of, 5–6
house-training of, 41–42
selection of, 7
socialization of, 9, 17–18
submission exercises for,
  25–26
Puppy Attitude Test, 7, 9–16

Q
Quiet, 94–95

R
Rally obedience, 89, 103
Recall game, 34, 60–61,
  64–66
Reinforcement, 21
Release, 49
Rescue dogs, 46, 96–101, 103
Restraint, 10, 12, 14
Retrieving, 10, 12, 15
Rope toy, 35

S
Safety, 20
Schutzhund, 88–89
Scruff, 26–27, 93
Settle, 26–27
Shaping behavior, 25
Showing, 85–86
Shunning, 47
Sight sensitivity, 10, 12, 15
Sit, 24, 35, 72
Sit-Stay, 52–54
Siwash harness, 80
Sleeping, 4
Social attraction, 11, 14
Social dominance, 10, 12, 14
Socialization, 9, 17–20, 91–92

Sound sensitivity, 10, 12, 15
Spaying, 9, 91
Specialty shows, 84
Stability, 10, 12, 14
Stacking, 85
Standard, 84
Stand for examination,
  63–64
Stand-stay, 57–58
Stationary attention, 48–50
Stay, 35, 52, 54–56, 58–59
Stimulation, 18
Strangers, 71
Stress, 18, 98
Subaortic stenosis, 6
Submission exercises, 25
Supervised separation, 73

T
Talking, 34–35
Temperament, 97
Therapy work, 88, 102–103
Timing, 34
Touch sensitivity, 10, 12, 15
Toys, 4, 31–33
Tracking, 86–87, 104
Treats, 33–34, 45, 61
Tug-enough command, 42–43
Tug games, 31, 33
Tug-O-War, 35
Tunnels, 77

V
Vari-Kennel, 39
Voice tone, 34–35
von Willebrand's disease, 6

W
Wagons, 79–80